BY THE SAME AUTHOR
Viet-Nam
Benedict Arnold: Hero and Traitor
Bolivar the Liberator
Captain John Smith and the Jamestown Story
Gentleman Johnny
Saladin: A Man for All Ages
The Assassins
The Terrorists
Witchcraft and the Mysteries
Mathilde Carré, Double Agent
The Invisible World of Espionage
The CIA at Work
Double Jeopardy
The Technology of Espionage

Britain's Intelligence Service

Lauran Paine

ROBERT HALE · LONDON

© *Lauran Paine 1979*
First published in Great Britain 1979

ISBN 0 7091 7622 8

Robert Hale Limited
Clerkenwell House
Clerkenwell Green
London EC1R 0HT

Set by Art Photoset Ltd.,
and printed in Great Britain
by Lowe & Brydone Ltd., Thetford, Norfolk.

Britain's Intelligence Service

Contents

Illustrations

PICTURE CREDITS

Radio Times Hulton Picture Library, 1, 2, 3, 4, 5, 6, 7; Popper-foto, 8, 9, 11, 12; Associated Press, 10.

1

Purposes And Policies

An Oxford scholar, Saul Rose, once noted that "Among the influences which shape the foreign policy of a country, geography appears as one of the most important and constant. Indeed it has been asserted that the 'geographical position of a nation is the chief factor in determining its foreign policy, and indeed the chief reason why it must have a foreign policy at all'."

Proceeding on the assumption that this is a valid rule of thumb, and applying it to that group of small islands lying a mere twenty miles from the European Continent, one almost immediately encounters that historic 'separateness' which has lent substance to the assertion that according to its geographical position Britain is not a part of Europe and can at will remain apart from Europe's affairs.

As a matter of historical fact the very insistence upon a separation between Britain and the Continent is rooted in the geographical proximity which since very early times has been a major consideration in British affairs. The desire to be separate is as constant as the geography which prohibits it.

Separate from the Continent or not, Britain from Roman times to the Hanoverian era was never free of masters who had one foot in Albion and the other foot in Europe. From Hanoverian times to the decade of the Second World War the economic and political affairs of Europe absolutely influenced, even dominated, the doctrines and policies of Great Britain.

No pair of human beings ever, so profoundly influenced British foreign policy from Hadrian's time to the present as did two foreigners, Napoleon Bonaparte and Adolf Hitler. Regardless of its favoured status as an 'island fortress', Britain, since the sixteenth century to its emergence as the United Kingdom was able to survive only because of the astuteness of its statesmen. These men recognized that as they guided an insular mercantile society into the role of foremost industrial power, their independence, their national survival, and their British identity depended upon a realistic appreciation that British foreign policy had to be based upon a relationship with foreigners. As the industrial society of the United Kingdom expanded in all directions in search of markets and raw materials, home-country policies had more and more to do with alien *ententes*, largely Continental, and less and less to do with British separateness. Only the British saw themselves as distinct from the other nations of Europe; no one else did including the Europeans.

The world-wide quest for wealth and strength brought Britain, most notably England, into all the ocean seas until a nation of European islanders became the formidable seamen of modern times. Because to a great degree all trade among Europeans, including those of the 'island fortress', had of necessity to be moved by sail, naval power had to be developed simultaneously with the fleets of trade and exploration, and once more, as a result of this far questing, British foreign policy reflected the relationships and the influences of foreigners. Being separate was not applicable; never in fact had been applicable. Geography in its narrowest context only dared to sponsor regional insularity before the days of sail, and that went back so far into history it could almost be maintained that for Britain there had never been any such thing as 'separateness' and while the intransigent British never stopped extolling their isolation, there was no such thing and really never had been. What there *was*, and what some mistook for isolation, was non-alignment. In 1887 the Prime Minister said that "No English Government can give an absolute guarantee for military and naval co-operation" and on the Continent this uniquely British doctrine was recognized by Prince Bismarck when he had occasion to comment upon "the absolute impossibility . . . [of depending upon] . . . alliances for which the [British] Crown are not answerable".

What had evolved over the centuries was a small European island-state capable of casting an inordinately large shadow, and this was made possible by foreign policies which retained vestiges of aloofness, which the British called 'separateness' and which other Europeans recognized as pure and simple non-alignment.

Occasionally through this policy the British demonstrated an uncanny omniscience. A considerable length of time elapsed before the other Europeans discovered that this was the result of an

Intelligence system which had developed along with colonialism, industrialization, and sea power.

More readily recognizable as an adjunct of the doctrine of non-alignment was the policy of avoiding entanglements on the Continent until someone's ambition sought through conquest to create a hegemony, then the British would support the *status quo* by "throwing . . . [their] weight now in this scale and now in that, but ever on the side opposed to the political dictatorship of the strongest single state or group at a given time".

In 1907 a junior official of the Foreign Office, Eyre Crowe, wrote a memorandum in which he defined the basic reason for non-alignment in these words: "The general character of England's foreign policy is determined by the immutable condition of her geographical situation on the ocean flank of Europe."

It was not possible to flesh out the bare bones of British foreign policy without, at the very least, an oblique reference to Europe.

Historically, it was easy to prove that according to the "immutable condition of geographical" fact, the British Isles were part of Europe. Yet because of that uncanny omniscience which time and again prevented Britain from being overrun when every one of her continental neighbours had been overrun at least once—some of them many times—it was just as easy to buttress the myth of 'separateness'. It existed, and to this day it exists, wholly fallible but intact.

As for that omniscience, British foreign policy was the visual and audible extension of skilful Intelligence operations which over many centuries made possible some glittering diplomatic successes —along with some of the most embarrassing gaffes in British history.

It might be well to remember that among all the nations which have influenced human destiny through historical events, none have embarked upon great adventures through war or peace without first employing the secret agencies all have maintained. Britain, for example, most certainly had spies accumulating information for her marcher lords well before the reign of the first Elizabeth, although almost nothing in the way of proof still exists.

The early history of Britain is a saga of fortified towns existing in an atmosphere of competition and frequent outright enmity, of enormous forests through which neighbours surely spied upon one another, and it is also a story of invasion, raids, and ultimately conquest, events which have historically lent themselves to the employment of secret services.

Actual evidence of espionage in those ancient times is at best sketchy; and except to demonstrate the need and therefore the existence of espionage a thousand years ago, there would be little value in detailing accomplishments which could have slight bearing upon the more sophisticated events—and Intelligence functions— of later times.

Indications of the existence of a national Intelligence organiz- ation in England were discernible early in the reign of Elizabeth I, when the realm of that remarkable woman, in the role of leader in world affairs, could hope to retain that lofty position only providing that English statesmen knew what alien monarchs and nations were contemplating.

Nor was this information-seeking restricted to the activities of opponents. In the search for markets, for raw materials, for strategic outposts and for allies, England, as a central figure in seagoing discovery and exploration, leaned more and more upon those in Crown service who, regardless of official designations, were purely and simply spies.

During the Elizabethan Age (roughly from 1558 the year of Elizabeth's accession to about 1640, a generation after her death) the known world, which had been divided in 1494 by the Pope between Spain and Portugal, consisted of enormous tracts of terri- tory labelled either 'Unknown' or 'Unexplored'. The interior of entire continents had yet to be visited by Protestant Europeans. Africa, most of North America, and Asia were scarcely more than blank silhouettes upon the charts of doughty navigators. Drake explored the New World shoreline in 1578–9 to spy upon the Spanish, and subsequently reported on all that he had seen, without any inkling of the enormous landmass lying beyond the misty mountains and the lowland seacoast fogs.

Francis Drake was not an outstanding spy. He was certainly not the first. Elizabeth's era was as notable for espionage as for explor- ation, with the distinction being that while one endeavour was trumpeted from one end of the land to the other, evidence of English prowess, the other accomplishment which traditionally was a secret function, was scarcely recognized outside the private chambers of its adherents, and they deliberately discouraged knowledge of its existence.

Throughout British history, to this day, historians have not even begun to put the Intelligence endeavour where it properly belongs —ahead of the diplomatic function.

Those who in ignorance, because general knowledge of British Intelligence has been such a zealously guarded secret, have maintained that the British have never been sufficiently Italianate to revel in *sub rosa* subtleties, might be astonished at how inaccurate that judgment has been. Some of the most accomplished secret agents of history have been Britons, beginning with Alfred, King of Wessex from 871 to 899, who toured the camps of his Danish adversaries disguised as a bard, gathering information concerning the strength and disposition of his enemies, and the peril they posed to his West Saxon realm.

From Alfred to Elizabeth I's 'Moor', swarthy Sir Francis Walsingham, on down through Britain's troubled generations to Cromwell's talented John Thurloe, many people—not always men —of manifold ingenuity have served their lords and their spy-masters with both exemplary dedication and some extraordinary results.

Few espionage networks throughout history have been as rich in tradition—or controversial accomplishments—as that of Great Britain. And none have been more zealous in guarding their secrecy.

It was this zealous secrecy which not only hindered even advantageous disclosures, but encouraged the myth of a feeble and inadequate network. However, since secrecy has always been to the Intelligence community what armaments have been to armies, nothing less than maximum confidentiality was acceptable either during the reign of the first Elizabeth, or during more recent past or present. In fact since medieval times in Britain it was the custom of spy-masters to disseminate deliberate disinformation of this particular variety in order to screen satisfactorily how efficient even those early systems were.

In 1668 Samuel Pepys wrote in his diary that on 27 December he

met Sir G. Downing, and walked with him for an hour, talking of business and how the late war was managed. . . . He told me that he had so good spies, that he hath the keys taken out of De Witt's pocket when he was abed, and his closet opened, and papers brought to him, and left in his hands for an [hour], and carried back and laid in their place again, and keys put into his pockets again. He said that he

has always their most private debates . . . brought to him . . . and an
hour after that . . . [hath] . . . sent word thereof to the King. . . .

Except for the Pepys' entry and a few, rare, similar disclosures
little of a genuinely revealing nature has survived to offer subsequent generations an insight into what even three centuries ago was
a good Intelligence system.

Excluding foreign sources which for obvious reasons have been
suspect, and including the Official Secrets Act of much later times,
penetration of the British Intelligence community has been made as
difficult as spy-masters could make it, the result being that, not
simply has very little been known, but of that very little, even less
has been allowed to reach print.

Yet between Pepys's era of the Restoration and Winston
Churchill's era of the Second World War, Britain's Intelligence
system managed in the main to avoid both enfeeblement and inade-
quacy, and when Churchill said that, "After twenty-five years
experience in peace and war, I believe the British Intelligence
Service to be the finest of its kind in the world," he had observed
both success and failure, had adjudged both, and was still able to
offer his eulogy.

Espionage—the total Intelligence environment—was regarded
by successive governments after that of Elizabeth I as being as
essential to the nation's survival as were ships and cannon. Few
nations developed as much versatility in their secret services as did
Britain, whose leaders recognized very early that major political
advantages accrued only to those who possessed a skilled, professional, information-gathering capability.

Nor did all nations surround their Intelligence facilities with such
a veritable thicket of obstacles against those, foe or friend, seeking
to achieve even a small degree of penetration. In the 1970s, most
reasonably informed individuals could name the chiefs of the
world's two largest Intelligence organizations—the CIA and the
KGB—and none of them could name the chief of Britain's
equivalent to those networks.

Even the name of the British organization whose purpose was
overseas espionage—M.I.6—was misleading, for while M.I.6
originally qualified as M. (military) I. (Intelligence) it ultimately
operated as an independent secret service whose responsibility was
espionage outside the country. For example, during the years from
1970 to 1975 external-service spies operated in the United States,

with tacit approval, in order to expose funds and arms being sent to embattled Ireland by United States citizens, mostly of Irish descent.

The counterpart of M.I.6 was M.I.5, which was generally concerned with counter-espionage; internal *sub rosa* investigations.

Ultimately M.I.6 became S.I.S, the Secret Intelligence Service, a designation which had been employed to categorize the rather numerous Second World War Intelligence networks of the army, navy, civilian official and allied agencies which were not only numerous but which until the invasion of Hitler's *Festung Europa* in June of 1944, literally stumbled over one another throughout the London area.

M.I.6, or S.I.S, had as its purpose the same concern which motivated espionage in Samuel Pepys's day—the accumulation of information which, when fed raw from the Intelligence sector to the hushed halls of high government emerged as the basis of all British foreign policy. The same policy, erudite proponents of political analysis had been contending down the decades, of necessity had to derive from Britain's geographical position, something which seemed at times to overlook or at least to minimize that much British history beyond the confines of home territories was the result of policies established by ambitious men in the furtherance of diplomatic schemes which seemed to be almost totally divorced from Britain's geography, or at the very best, had only a very distant and morganatic relationship to it.

But fortunately when Britain, more than her two nearest European rivals, France and Germany, emerged from the Elizabethan Age vigorously and fully committed to involvement in every corner of the world, she possessed an Intelligence capability equal to every challenge. Otherwise very clearly she could scarcely have managed some of the outstanding achievements which marked British accomplishments during the nation's greatest crises, and although success was tempered by some resounding failures the system remained alive and well, and it is still alive and well.

2

God's Clear Design

It may not be entirely inappropriate at this juncture to go back some 390 years in order to chronicle the Intelligence aspect of two particularly stirring events which were never afterwards detailed from the Intelligence point of view, although each was examined, and continues to be examined, from other points of view.

One of these events was the tragedy of Mary Stuart, Queen of Scots. The other, greater in many aspects, certainly more awesome and spectacular was the affair of *La Felicissima Armada,* the Most Fortunate Fleet.

When the official Spanish list became known, and the full awesome strength of that enormous flotilla could be appreciated, someone inevitably added 'invincible'. It became *La Invencible Armarda,* and after disaster struck, Spanish irony insisted that the designation *Invencible* remain; and remain it has down to our time.

During the Elizabethan era there were other instances which helped reveal how early English Intelligence systems operated but there was never throughout the whole of English history another Queen of Scots nor another Invincible Armada although in the latter regard, roughly two centuries later, the French under Bonaparte considered a sea-borne invasion of Albion, and 350 years later the Germans under *Reichsführer* Hitler posed a more direct threat—a topic which will recur later—but no other enemy of Britain ever filled the Channel with such an invasion complement as did Spain's Catholic Majesty Philip II.

Nor did the certainty of success ever rest so tantalizingly close at hand. In the year 1558 when Elizabeth Tudor came to the throne at twenty-five years of age England was not a power to be envied and neither was her Tudor monarch. The treasury was bare, the currency debased, there was no army, Elizabeth's throne was tottering, England's navy consisted of freebooters such as Francis

Drake, no better than brigands, and Elizabeth's impoverished subjects were divided, uncertain and demoralized. They had recently
lost the realm's last toehold on the Continent and in the process
had been soundly beaten by the French. Calais, that relic of
Plantagenet glory had reverted to triumphant France.

As for Elizabeth who had matured in the shadow of the heads-
man's axe, she had her throne but without a friend or an ally on the
Continent and with enemies to spare, abroad and at home.

Finally, this perverse, often cruel and always penurious woman,
with less right to the throne of England than almost any of her
predecessors, was to rule alone, an unmarried woman, and was to
successfully dominate an ambitious, predatory nobility, along with
one of the most notoriously discontented, unruly and cantankerous
populaces in Europe—or anywhere else. As though these were not
a sufficient challenge, she chose also to defy the most powerful
monarch of her time, Philip of Spain, whose vast fleet and great
armies were everywhere as conquerors, and she had not even a
standing army, only some itinerant guardsmen, while her fleet was
less even than a pirate's covey.

Elizabeth had as diplomat and secretary Francis Walsingham
who created for her an Intelligence organization subsequent
chroniclers were to call "omnipresent", "vastly skilled", and of
"considerable size", which was unsurpassed for its adroitness.
However, as a matter of fact, it was never large, for many years
consisting of less than a dozen full-time agents and at its peak
utilizing the services of no more than fifty people including part-
time volunteer informers, who, when paid at all, commonly
received their reimbursement from Sir Francis because of the
Virgin Queen's parsimony.

Walsingham was the ideal individual to assist his queen steer her
very uncertain course through the storms and shoals of an era of
unequalled social and political turbulence.

The many plots originating among the Catholic powers of the
Continent, all of whom were her sworn enemies, either to coerce
Elizabeth back to the papal fold or to destroy her, were thwarted by
Sir Francis's ceaseless vigilance. At the same time he penetrated the
camps and palaces of Elizabeth's enemies with great success, and at
home in Britain was largely instrumental in bringing to the execu-
tioner's block his queen's most formidable competitor, Mary
Stuart, Queen of Scots.

Elizabeth was well aware of her perilous condition, although history has not troubled to explain how fully aware she really was. Walsingham's agents on the Continent, in the court of the French monarch and discreetly in place throughout Spain and Portugal, sent back coded reports of the seemingly endless Catholic plots to assassinate her, or to widen the division in Britain between Elizabeth and Mary, Queen of Scots.

In the latter case the clear peril was that sufficient disruption might be created to allow an invasion of Britain, perhaps through Scotland, utilizing any of the invincible hosts of France or Spain. It was conceivable that an allied force from both Catholic powers might be used, but there was rarely enough agreement between them for such a thing to actually happen.

In any event the immediate danger to Elizabeth was not just a dagger in the back, but also a breach in the defensive shoreline of her homeland, things which Mary, Queen of Scots was certainly capable of encouraging.

The proof which history has largely ignored but which neither Elizabeth nor Francis Walsingham neglected came forth in a series of secret documents concocted by Mary's chief plotters Anthony Babington and her secretary Gilbert Curll.

One of Walsingham's best secret agents was Thomas Phelippes, who became not only a spy in the queen's service while very young, but who developed into England's first outstanding cryptanalyst. It was Phelippes who put before Sir Francis Walsingham the conspiracy's decoded secret letters which were of such an incriminating nature as to guarantee the execution of Mary.

Phelippes could decode from French, Latin, Italian and Spanish. He broke the ciphers used by Spain's envoys thus allowing Walsingham to keep Elizabeth informed of every Spanish plot against her. Phelippes travelled widely on the Continent gleaning valuable facts to be transmitted to London. Any event likely to have a bearing upon Elizabeth, and any scheme involving peril to her realm was ferreted out by Phelippes and reported. But where Walsingham and his chief agent excelled at home was in collaborating to eliminate the nearer of Elizabeth's perils and the way they accomplished it was through the employment of a classical Intelligence ploy.

Sir Francis was certain Elizabeth's cousin was either hand in glove with the conspirators or was a tacit bystander in their plots. Subsequent historians reported that "There was no proof of her complicity in these plots", but facts suggested otherwise, and Sir Francis set in motion his scheme to prove either that Mary *was* a conspirator, or was at the very least the lodestone which attracted his queen's violent enemies.

He dispatched one of his agents, a man named Gilbert Gifford, to Mary's residence, the castle of Chartley, for the purpose of penetrating Mary's household.

Gifford was an example of that type of member of the Intelligence business who has over the centuries proved less than admirable, personally, while at the same time providing his employers with excellent information. As an English Catholic he was already in difficulties when Walsingham recruited him. In exchange for Walsingham's protection, Gifford agreed to become a spy. It was as simple as that; there were no emotional aspects of patriotism involved, no lofty principles. Gifford spied zealously— and successfully—against Elizabeth's most formidable rival in Britain, to avoid trouble for himself.

In due course he became a confidant of Mary's chief plotter Anthony Babington and from that moment Mary's fate was in Walsingham's hands.

The fact that both Mary, Queen of Scots and Babington accepted Walsingham's agent for what he professed to be—a dedicated zealot in Mary's cause willing to die to prove it—was partly due to Gilbert Gifford's undoubted ability as an actor. Down the years hundreds of martyrs have been duped by the same variety of secret agent.

Gifford secured the critical position of messenger, and in this role was confronted with one of those unique situations many secret agents encounter. Mary was under house-arrest at Chartley. Elizabeth's guards watched not only Mary and her entourage, but censored letters and were particularly interested in everything which was sent out of Chartley. Gifford devised a means for getting the plotters' correspondence safely away by concealing it in beer kegs.

But his purpose, as clever as it appeared to the plotters, was not to expedite delivery of Mary's correspondence to her supporters on the Continent and elsewhere, it was to make certain that this clearly incriminating information reached Sir Francis Walsingham, and the codes Mary's people used went with it so that Walsingham's cryptanalyst, Thomas Phelippes, could lay bare every word which was written.

The greatest windfall was when Gifford was entrusted with a hoard of secret correspondence from the Continent delivered to him by the French ambassador. Much of this material—all of it highly incriminating—had been accumulating for almost two years because prior to the advent of Gifford there was no way to get it past the guards into Chartley.

Gifford allowed for some additional delay. He took the entire hoard to Walsingham where it was all duly decoded, read, copied, then re-sealed and 'smuggled' into Chartley *via* the beer-barrel route.

From this source as well as others which Walsingham successfully exploited emerged the facts which doomed Mary. There was a well-organized plot to assassinate Elizabeth (and Walsingham too, who was known and feared by Elizabeth's enemies). After the death of Elizabeth and her Master of Intelligence one of Spain's great armies was to make certain Mary was placed upon the English throne.

Walsingham's Intelligence was so complete that he could name the six assassins—all English courtiers—who were to stab Elizabeth to death, but there was a particular difficulty. The names of those six men were in code, and because each name was more nearly an individual pseudonym—a play upon an actual name and therefore not susceptible to code keys—not even Thomas Phelippes could give Walsingham the real names.

Sir Francis was an individual of exceptional perspicacity. After a reasonable interlude of preparing a trap, during which time he forged a footnote in code to one of the ingoing letters to Chartley requesting the "names and qualities of the six gentlemen which are to accomplish" the assassination, he also arranged for Anthony Babington to dine with one of his secret agents, and to have a copy of a warrant for Babington's arrest 'carelessly' lying nearby for Babington to see.

Babington saw the warrant and predictably sought to flee, and in so doing the six courtiers were also alerted. They too fled. All seven men were apprehended, all seven were convicted on the strength of Walsingham's damning evidence, and all seven were executed.

But Walsingham's greater coup was Mary, Queen of Scots herself. In order to assure her permanent removal he first had to have solid proof that, contrary to allegations of future historians that no proof existed against Mary, she actually knew the details of the assassination plot, and approved of them.

He set a bait for Mary by forwarding to her a letter from Anthony Babington in which the plot against Elizabeth was clearly detailed. Then he had to anxiously await Mary's reply. It came, eventually, was placed before him, and, over Mary's signature was full acknowledgement of the "enterprise", plus advice on how to "bring it to good success".

Without doubt Mary knew of the plot, encouraged the plotters, and ardently wanted Elizabeth's assassination to succeed. On 8 February 1587 Mary, Queen of Scots was beheaded. Walsingham had succeeded in protecting his queen, but in so doing he had further inflamed her enemies across the Channel something he certainly had anticipated, but these other enemies were at least out in the open. Since they were already committed to Elizabeth's downfall, by eliminating Mary he had, if anything, eliminated the clearer danger of secret peril in order to be able to concentrate more fully upon the overt peril. This was of course captained by that enigmatic, gloomy man Philip II in his hermitical Escorial who, as monarch of reunited Spain ruled more of the earth's surface than anyone else since the Beginning.

Elizabeth and her 'Moor', Walsingham, had excellent reason to fear unsmiling Philip, who owned more titles, fiefdoms and duchies than there were English markets, but rashly or not they did not fear him. The queen's courage was steadfast and her shrewdness, which would become increasingly manifest as time passed, proved to be the ideal counter-balance. She was the precise check-rein for Walsingham. She was beguiling, amazingly perceptive, never entirely predictable and altogether an incredible monarch as well as a fascinating woman. She possessed a will of iron cloaked behind her female frailties. She was immovable in conviction and completely calm in dangerous adversity.

Sir Francis on the other hand was a swarthy, slight, nervous and energetic man of immense cleverness, talent and guile. An individual of powerful Puritan convictions who saw in Catholicism the worst of all perils to humanity. Walsingham consistently and impatiently urged Elizabeth to make war against the tentacles of Rome wherever they existed.

He was willing to scheme against the greatest empire of all time from a cluttered small office upon a small, troubled island, daring the armed hosts of Spain's formidable Alexander Farnese, Duke of Parma, and his mighty uncle, Don Juan of Austria, both of whom outspokenly championed the invasion of England. Further he encouraged Elizabeth in her obvious delight in sending her sea-going freebooters to singe Philip's beard.

Fortunately for these two individuals, Elizabeth the Virgin Queen and Sir Francis Walsingham her spy-master, he was never able to persuade her against her better judgment, and she was never able to lessen his zeal in her service by refusing funds when he most needed them. He nearly bankrupted himself to serve and protect her, while she moved through all the thickets of her long reign with consummate skill, the perfect foil to Walsingham's occasional bursts of recklessness, while he was in turn the perfect tool for her artifices.

In the wise words of G. M. Trevelyan: "If Elizabeth had taken Walsingham's advice on every occasion she would have been ruined. If she had never taken it she would have been ruined no less. On the whole she took what was best."

She was not to be the last national leader whose absolute faith in an Intelligence organization was fortunately tempered by a variety of judgment which could dare with caution, which could take chances with discretion, and which could heighten the morale of a spy-master while at the same time avoiding entanglements which would have drained the slim resources of a poor realm.

But she *would* dare. When England's great nationalist William Cecil opposed the piratical sweeps of such sea-dogs as Francis Drake on the grounds that England could produce no really adequate defence against Philip's certain retaliation, Her Majesty listened instead to Francis Walsingham who encouraged those harassing expeditions regardless of a woeful lack of defences. "So it is," she exclaimed, "that I would gladly be revenged on the King of Spain", and very discreetly through her spy-master bought shares in Drake's enterprise of purest piracy.

The result was precisely what Cecil feared. Philip's retaliation, however, probably had much less to do with the annoying activities of Elizabeth's freebooters than it had to do with the beheading of Mary, Queen of Scots, among other purely political matters. In any case Cecil's fears would have come to pass eventually since Philip's clear duty as Defender of the Faith was to smite heretics, and in that momentous decade of the 1580s when the idea of a vast fleet sailing against England was first mentioned, to the time of its stunning and disastrous defeat, Elizabeth and her spy-master Walsingham were required to strain to their utmost in order to put out a fire they themselves had ignited. Fortunately for them and for England it was God's clear design that they should both be equal to it.

3

Disparo!

The issues that later statesmen considered grounds for justifiable conflict, such as trade routes, strategic enclaves, resources, and pure economics, were certainly present in the year the Virgin Queen and her cousin, Philip of Spain, finally clashed, but they were not the main issues; those consisted of elements later generations deemed totally unfit to fight about, such as royal succession, incompatible social mores, and religious ideas. No one fought for God after the close of the Middle Ages, and those who professed otherwise, lied; they might *say* they warred in defence of faith but examination revealed an economic interest, an Imperial desire, a need for free access to resources.

In 1588 Philip and Elizabeth warred over conflicting religious ideas. Philip more than Elizabeth; he was always devout, she was occasionally so, depending upon her needs of the moment. His was a compartmentalized, unhurried, almost stolid yet infinitely detailed and capable mind. Elizabeth was sceptical, coolly analytical, rarely susceptible to enthusiasm, disenchanted. She could never, not to save her realm nor her life, have consented to create an armada. Her cousin could never have learned to know his subjects as she knew hers.

They were not personal enemies. He admired many things about Elizabeth and she sought more to annoy him, to keep herself perpetually in his thoughts, than to ruin him, although neither would have shed many tears over the end of the other.

What Philip needed for the sake of his immortal soul was to bring England back to Catholicism. He would exhaust the resources of the world's largest empire to accomplish, what to later generations would seem shocking, outrageous, and absolutely absurd.

When he initially entertained some idea of a great invasion fleet Francis Walsingham had the information almost at once and

England's shipmasters had it shortly after, or as quickly as Walsingham could send it to them. Drake being Walsingham's favourite, and to some extent also his confidant and agent, when Drake appealed to his queen for permission—and support—in a raid down the Spanish coast, Walsingham lent his influence. Elizabeth was persuaded but without great enthusiasm, and Drake began at once to put together a fleet of good ships including four superb galleons plus several swift pinnaces.

It required considerable time to organize such a flotilla. Not the least of Drake's worries was desertion. Sailors who normally fought to sail with a successful plunderer because their percentage of loot could establish them in comfort for years, heard rumours that this time Drake was not sailing to plunder and raid, he was rather putting forth to fight, and that was a different matter. The advantages were not only certain to be less, but the dangers were very great, especially when the rumours had it that Drake intended to sail right into the Spaniard's harbours.

Drake wrote to Walsingham when he was finally ready to sail: "I thank God I find no man but as all members of one body to stand for our gracious Queen and country against Antichrist and his members . . . If your honour did now see the fleet under sail and know with what resolution men's minds do enter into this action, as your honour would rejoice to see them, so you would judge a small force would not divide them."

Drake sailed, and Walsingham's discreet hand was faintly visible throughout all Drake's hasty preparations and early departure. (He was not fully provisioned, nor manned on some vessels.)

Walsingham's encouragement had behind it events which Drake could only have suspected. Elizabeth, for example, was in correspondence with Alexander Farnese, Duke of Parma, Philip II's most formidable general. She in fact had been in correspondence with him for some time and now at last their wary exchange had begun to seem more cautiously open and hopeful. Would Elizabeth at the last moment have chosen to restrain Drake from his clearly provocative descent upon Spain's coastlands in order not to jeopardize her dialogue with Parma? Not, one suspects, if Sir Francis Walsingham could prevent it. So Drake put to sea in haste. "Our ships are under sail," he wrote to Walsingham. "God grant we may so live in His fear as the enemy may have cause to say God doth fight for Her Majesty as well abroad as at home. Haste!"

Haste indeed. Walsingham's undoubted insistence upon it made all the difference. Drake was under sail when a courier arrived at Plymouth Harbour with a royal command that Drake "forbear to enter forcibly into any of the said King's ports or havens, or to offer violence to any of his towns or shipping within harbouring, or to do any act of hostility upon the land". On the other hand, with an interest in any plundering enterprise, Elizabeth was willing to add in the same correspondence that it was quite all right for Drake to "get into your possession such shipping of the said King or his subjects as you shall find at sea".

Drake was spared the humiliation as well as the exasperation. He did not receive those royal commands. Why he did not is a minor mystery. The command was sent down *nine days after Drake had sailed.* Surely under ordinary circumstances news between Plymouth Harbour and Greenwich where the countermanding order originated did not require nine days in transit. In fact Philip's capable ambassador Bernardo de Mendoza heard *in Paris* that Drake had sailed, before the privy councillors at Greenwich sent down the order. Had someone, again, intervened in Drake's—and Walsingham's—favour?

Also, when the order was sent forth in pursuit of Drake aboard a swift pinnace, the captain had clearly been informed that his mission was not compellingly urgent, otherwise he probably would not have still been beating back and forth in the Channel until he encountered a prize Portuguese merchantman, after which he forgot all about the countermanding order, and his original mission which was to deliver it.

But Philip's Intelligence organization was even larger and better financed than Elizabeth's. He received coded dispatches announcing Drake's departure from Plymouth Harbour with thirty ships on 12 April 1587. These messages set forth clearly Drake's intentions and his probable course at sea.

Bernardo de Mendoza wrote a personal assessment which was on target. Drake, he reported to his king, was certainly going to raid Cadiz Harbour where Philip's supply vessels were at anchor, the purpose being to sow such havoc and disruption as to destroy schedules, as well as much shipping as possible.

Philip did not read Mendoza's letter the day it arrived. He was incapacitated with gout. There was nothing to be done in any case. Eighteen days out of Plymouth Harbour, Drake had Cadiz in sight.

It was a fine, clear, golden Wednesday afternoon, 29 April. He sailed in, caught the Spaniards completely by surprise, caused such a panic in the city that shrieking townspeople trampled thirty of their numbers to death including small children as they choked narrow roadways in an attempt to escape the town, and as guns began sending forth shock-waves, Drake's onslaught began.

Before the attack was finished the English had destroyed "about thirty" vessels great and small. (Confidential Intelligence reports to Philip listed losses as twenty-four ships valued at 172,000 ducats.) But the purpose of the raid, to deprive Spain of material which was at Cadiz Harbour on its way to Lisbon where Philip's armada was being ponderously put together, was rather satisfactorily concluded.

It was anything but a death-blow, however. Philip deplored the losses but was not too concerned with any delay they might cause. On the other hand he was impressed enough to say that while "The loss was not very great . . . the daring of the attempt was great indeed."

Sir Francis Drake who had seen enough to also be impressed with Philip's preparations, wrote a report to Walsingham which included a description of the raid, and then said: "I assure your honour the like preparation was never heard of nor known as the King of Spain hath and daily maketh to invade England . . . which if they be not impeaded before they join will be very perilous . . . all possible preparations for defence are very expedient. . . . Prepare in England strongly and most by sea!"

Another report of the Cadiz affair to reach Walsingham was from an agent named Wychegerde, a North German, whose cover as a grain and sundries merchant was actually his trade, since spying for Elizabeth was not a financially rewarding occupation.

In this instance Wychegerde smarted doubly for his sympathies. He lost a cargo of corn in the hold of a ship Drake sank at Cadiz, and he only very belatedly received any thanks from Walsingham who kept the North German constantly moving among the Spanish towns, camps and garrisons, gleaning information.

Once he was taken by pirates, relieved of all his commodities as well as his last coin, even his clothing, and was freed at Boulogne in his underwear.

It was this spy who kept Walsingham informed of Spain's successes and problems in the Lowlands, and who also, incidentally, spied on the English forces aiding the Dutch. From Wychegerde's reports a clear picture began to emerge. While Philip's pre-occupation with his great invasion armada ensured steady progress, Parma's triumphant strides over the Lowlands added greatly to the dangers facing England. If Parma's host was poised along the Flemish coast opposite England, and Philip's Invincible Armada arrived to take Parma aboard, unless a miracle occurred Elizabeth was lost, and so also was her realm.

Walsingham had to know Parma's strength. Accordingly tough and resolute Wychegerde went forth in a lawless environment where even disciplined soldiers stealthily robbed and murdered at night, where no one was safe not even Spanish generals. He plodded through the marshes counting Spaniards and ultimately forwarded his coded report. Parma had five thousand Spaniards, Walloons, Germans and Italians. A few more, a few less, but five thousand ready and able.

Previous English estimates by such notables as Robert Dudley, Earl of Leicester who commanded in the Lowlands, put Parma's force as high as eighteen thousand men. They were not inclined to believe Wychegerde's figure, and yet in Parma's secret correspon-dence with Philip, Wychegerde's estimate was proven accurate. The difficulty arose from the fact that no one realized just how accurate Wychegerde's figure was until long afterwards. At the time, Walsingham had no access to Parma's secret dispatches.

Wychegerde also penned a flat statement about those five thousand veterans which suggested why, to Spain's enemies, those troops seemed three times as numerous as they were.

They were Parma's best, most seasoned, vigilant and valiant soldiers. Although in Lowland mud to their hocks, under dismal pelting rainfall with the guns of Parma's enemies trained on them from above, they cursed and turned sullen, they never missed an opportunity, scorned needless risks, and could be neither panicked nor surprised. "They maintain great order," Wychegerde reported, "their chief strength lies in the carefulness of their watch and the prudence of their methods by day and by night."

Walsingham took time to assess Parma's numbers, as well as what appeared to be his strategy. The Spanish were meeting stubborn resistance at Bruges and Sluys.

Then Wychegerde forwarded another report: judging from the manner in which the defenders used their weapons, they were probably running short of powder and lead.

But Walsingham had time. He knew that a fleet and soldiers were on their way to succour the Dutch and their allies, and whatever the outcome of that incessant manoeuvring among the marshes and estuaries of the Netherlands, the overshadowing peril remained constant for England: Parma's army, ready to be ferried across the Channel, and Philip's seagoing accumulation at Lisbon, which was to ferry it.

No English city had modern fortifications and according to many who were in a position to know the English were neither as seasoned nor as united as Parma's host, and therefore a conquest would be easier for Parma once he reached England, than his conquests in Zeeland and Holland had been. But first he had to be put ashore.

Walsingham's judgment of Parma, the greatest captain of his age, and Parma's troops, who had consistently beaten every adversary, could not afford to be inaccurate, nor was it. If Parma reached England, Elizabeth Tudor and her isle were lost.

Walsingham concentrated on accumulating information on Philip's armada and the picture to emerge was even more breathtaking than was Parma's image.

Philip had available to him all the seagoing resources of the Mediterranean. To his own navy he could add the second most powerful Atlantic fleet, that of Portugal, Spain's neighbour which had yielded to Philip and was now one of his duchies. He could also add fleets from France and Italy, captured ships from the Lowlands, vessels from his ingratiating allies. It was early knowledge among the Intelligence sector that Philip's fleet would number perhaps as many as one hundred and fifty ships, a staggering armada.

Walsingham's Intelligence files had a different number.

Philip had requested from his greatest admiral, Don Alvaro de Bazán, the Marquis of Santa Cruz, an estimate of the naval requirements he would need against England. Santa Cruz, like Parma, never once belittled the English. His reply was that the enterprise would require one hundred and fifty great ships (battleships), forty large, heavily armed *urcas* (supply ships), plus three hundred and twenty support vessels in all categories as well as swift and deadly *fregatas* and *zabras* (armed light cruisers), forty row-galleys and six *galleasses* (three-masted warship with cannon on both sides).

The total was five hundred and ten sail.

Added to this was Santa Cruz's estimate of thirty thousand

mariners to serve this fleet, plus supplies and billets above and below all decks to accommodate over sixty thousand soldiers of an invasion force.

There had never been such a force anywhere near the English Channel. Walsingham could only have read those figures with incredulity.

Santa Cruz's estimate also called for tons of pikes, corselets, arquebuses, powder and shot, ropes (and slings to take aboard horses—no Spanish army went anywhere on foot if it could possibly avoid doing so), as well as hundreds of barrels of oil, salt fish, biscuits and all manner of incidentals, besides tons of provender for men and animals.

Santa Cruz's estimate included an idea that the swift conquest many had predicted would not be so swift. Like Parma, he knew the English, having fought them before. Santa Cruz's estimate of requirements was based upon a campaign to last eight months, possibly even a year.

Philip's prudent deliberations left him staring at a cost-estimate Walsingham no doubt had also arrived at: three million eight hundred thousand ducats. *Disparo!* Nonsense. He did not have it. Nor had it been Philip's intention to accept the Santa Cruz estimate by itself.

He had asked Parma to also consider requirements for the enterprise of England, and this time the cost was agreeably negligible. Parma the greatest land general of his generation made Santa Cruz blanch. He did not need an armada. All he wanted was thirty thousand infantry, four thousand cavalry, and a sufficient force of barges to ferry them across to England from Nieuport and Dunkirk in France, the crossing to be made in a single night. (Centuries later both Napoleon and Hitler adopted Parma's idea verbatim—with identical results.)

If Philip took pleasure from Parma's estimate over that of Santa Cruz, most certainly Walsingham also did. To ferry across that great host of soldiers would require not less than eight or nine hundred barges. Walsingham's spies in France would have no difficulty at all keeping watch over such an accumulation. England's tough navy could drown the lot. Parma's superiority on land obviously did not extend beyond the surf.

Walsingham had reason to hope Parma's plan would be adopted. However, neither Parma nor Santa Cruz were spared the annotated

Disparo! Philip saw at once the fallacy of both schemes and came up with one of his own, which was all he had probably intended from the beginning, and by the time Walsingham had his coded copy Philip's plan was under way.

Parma was to collect barges and be ready on the Flemish coast for Santa Cruz's arrival by sea. Parma would be reinforced from other Spanish armies although probably not to the extent he wished.

The Armada would sail from Lisbon, (not Spain as Santa Cruz had advocated), take Parma aboard and properly cross the Channel under an adequate umbrella of guns. It sounded simple. It was just not that simple to *do*, however, and Philip's accumulation of ships was beset with one inconvenience after another as the months dragged along.

Walsingham's spies were in Lisbon as well as Madrid and Cadiz. In late 1587 they reported that *La Invencible Armada* was preparing to sail. He went at once to inform the queen. She had already vetoed Sir John Hawkins' suggestion for a naval blockade of the Spanish coast.

She certainly did not entertain any illusion about the purpose of Philip's Armada, although he had enjoined secrecy regarding its ultimate destination, had even encouraged deceptive rumours. But as a matter of fact Walsingham's intimation that the Armada was coming in December of 1587 was wrong to the extent of five months. It did not appear in the Channel until the summer of 1588, and by that time his spies had given Elizabeth a complete inventory of what was coming, and she had finally—very belatedly according to Hawkins, Drake and Walsingham—opened her purse for England's seagoing line of defence.

Coastal defences were not overlooked. Armed militia were established along with companies of watchers on the hills and headlands who were to signal with great bonfires when a Spanish sail was sighted, but knowledgeable Englishmen believed the issue would be resolved on water, not land. Sir Francis Walsingham, along with others of Her Majesty's officialdom, most notably Sir John Hawkins, had, since the clear fact of eventual conflict was forced upon them, and through the long seasons of Spain's procrastination, brought to full strength not the largest navy in Atlantic waters but quite possibly the best. It consisted of eighteen bristling galleons, the smallest of three hundred tons, seven additional galleons of roughly one hundred tons, a host of swift pinnaces along with support and supply vessels to match, and crews of excellent morale—which was not always the case aboard English war vessels.

England was as ready by May of 1588 as she could be, but Philip who had enjoyed a more lengthy period of preparations, was not. In fact at his impatient insistence Santa Cruz finally agreed to sail forth, but one week before the day he was to sail out of Lisbon, Alvaro de Bazán, Marquis of Santa Cruz went to bed on 9 February and died.

Philip was ready for that emergency too. He appointed the elfin, charming Duke of Medina Sidonia to Santa Cruz's admiralship. Medina Sidonia was Captain General of Andalusia. He was in no way qualified to become an Admiral of the Ocean Sea, except by Philip's appointment, which was enough.

Medina Sidonia—Don Alonso de Guzman el Bueno—could not believe it. He begged to be relieved of the responsibility even before setting out for Lisbon. He caught cold at sea, he said, was seasick as well. Additionally, he knew nothing of naval matters, nor for that matter, of war.

Philip remained steadfast and Medina Sidonia went to Lisbon, had the enterprise blessed and re-blessed, had his soldiers and sailors confessed (and enjoined against blasphemy until after the conquest of England), went aboard and sailed from Lisbon Harbour in the second week of May. Because swift couriers were faster than sails which did not always billow when they should, Sir Francis Walsingham knew by the third week of May, that the Armada was coming. He also knew of the death of Santa Cruz and the appointment of Medina Sidonia, but most importantly he had the Spaniard's inventory, had in fact possessed it for some time. Philip's fleet of five hundred first class war vessels had diminished to about one hundred and thirty sail in all categories. Among the great fighting vessels Medina Sidonia did not noticeably outmatch the English and his largest vessel, an Italian carrack, would have brought bleak smiles to his enemies' faces. It was so large and clumsy and unmanageable as to pose a greater threat to the Spaniards among whom it would be required to manoeuvre than the English.

Walsingham's agents had fulfilled their duties well. Elizabeth and her councillors were finally able to make an appraisal and come up with more than a line of battle, with also a very great hope for victory. They also had an opportunity to double check. They had Walsingham's Intelligence report, and while Medina Sidonia was delayed in Portugal by unexpected bad weather, he passed the time drawing up his own inventory. Not just of ships and men, but of guns, powder and shot, medical supplies, casks of wine and salt fish, priests (180), biscuits, cheese, rice, oil, and beans—and he had this published. Philip's confidential affair had never been secret anyway.

Nineteen days out of Lisbon, on 19 June, at Corunna Harbour where The Invincible Armada put in to replenish its supply of drinking water, the weather created havoc again, this time in the middle of the night, howling with such fury the Armada was scattered like chaff.

On 24 June the limping ships rendezvoused—thirty ships were now unaccounted for, which was a serious blow, not only for the loss of war vessels but because six thousand mariners and soldiers were upon those ships.

For a month while repairs were made and spies sent hasty reports to England of the Armada's plight, Medina Sidonia and his monarch exchanged letters. The duke's words were gloomy. Philip's words were dogged. Medina Sidonia was to get on with it. Finally, as the last of the lost vessels came in, Medina Sidonia struck out again. It was now late July.

Spanish light vessels coursing ahead found no trace of English ships, which may have been a relief to some—those who feared Drake as they feared *Señor Satán*—but to the members of Medina Sidonia's Intelligence corps it meant something different. Were the English, then, waiting up ahead in full strength?

In the early morning of 29 July an English captain, Thomas Fleming, one of Her Majesty's seagoing watchdogs in the Channel, reported a sighting of Spanish sails off the Scilly Isles. By mid-afternoon the admirals had been alerted, and indeed the English had been chafing for months.

Walsingham's work was done. Now it was up to *El Draque*, Lord Admiral Charles Howard, his seventy-year-old brother William, Lord Mayor of Plymouth, a taut clique of captains and their sea-dogs who for the most part had been standing by at their own expense.   At nightfall Elizabeth's heaviest ships sailed out of Plymouth Harbour on the ebbing tide with a moderate wind. In the morning freshets the balance of the vessels went forth.

On Saturday, 30 July, the Spaniards overhauled and captured an English fisherman who told them what lay ahead: a reinforced Royal Navy. Their first encounter occurred when a mosquito-like

English pinnace darted under the towering stern of a mighty Spaniard, *La Rata*, and was fired upon with annoyance. The pinnace popped back with her much smaller guns and scuttled away.

Then the English caught sight of Philip's array of might coming steadily on, a wall of ships, banners aloft, considerably fewer than five hundred but still an awesome sight.

An English squadron seeking to slip past exchanged shots, which were heard on the hushed and crowded shoreline. Medina Sidonia ordered the signal gun fired. His warships eased up into battle positions, forming a precise crescent. The English, with more manoeuvrable vessels, were impressed. They were standing to battle in a nearly straight rank. The Spaniards called it *en ala*.

The initial shots announcing this historic opening of modern sea-warfare's first engagement were lost in a deafening exchange between the Lord Admiral's *Ark Royal* and Don Alonso de Leiva's *Rata Coronada*. They pounded one another with broadside after broadside.

Drake, Frobisher and Hawkins attacked the Spaniard's flanks. The battle was eagerly joined and at once the basic difference between Mediterranean and Atlantic naval tactics became evident. The Spaniards, whose purpose was to come to grips with an enemy man to man, whose entire strategy was based upon getting close enough to grapple and board, were aboard ships which were nothing less than floating fortresses. Huge, towering vessels designed to take aboard thousands of soldiers; to stand and hurl broadside after broadside. They were not readily manoeuvrable.

Lord Admiral Charles Howard's fleet on the other hand had been rebuilt, manned and outfitted so that each captain could fight with *his ship*, not his men. They were lower to the water, faster, more sensitive to the tiller and not top-heavy. In the Channel, even without the fire-ships which were eventually set ablaze and sent against the Armada scattering Spaniards like quail, or the bad weather, the boldness of the English and the superior manoeuvrability of their warships would have established naval precedence. The English ships were better in the Channel, and with something like parity of numbers were almost certain to succeed.

At the close of the first day a Spanish report noted that while Medina Sidonia "collected the fleet he could do little more" because the English "ships are so fast and nimble they can do anything they like with them".

Nonetheless upon the other side England's captains had reason to be apprehensive. For all their salvoes the enemy's great ships had suffered only superficial injuries, his discipline was perfect and he was still full of fight after nightfall ended the initial meeting.

Now too, Philip's Armada was set to course ahead to its rendezvous with Parma. The Lord Admiral wrote to Walsingham that, "We gave them fight from nine o'clock until one and made some of them to bear room to stop their leaks, notwithstanding we durst not adventure to put in among them, their fleet being so strong."

But *after* the battle of the twenty-first, Medina Sidonia lost two capital ships. One, the *San Salvador* exploded. Apparently her gunpowder magazine had blown up. The other war vessel, the flagship of Pedro de Valdes, the *Nuestra Señora del Rosaria* collided with a second vessel, lost her bowsprit and was incapacitated. That same night the weather began to change noticeably and by the following morning the Channel and beyond were dismally grey and filled with an ominously running sea.

The English were in pursuit, the Spaniards on their massive way up the Channel—the weather was abating—and after another day-long engagement—during which the English took prizes and prisoners and their war fleet was reinforced, the weather again appeared to be threatening. By Tuesday morning with a wind from the east the battle was joined at close encounter "with confusion enough", as one contemporary chronicler put it. The Spaniards tried to grapple and board, the English tried to stand clear and fire broadsides. Time and again the Spaniards either sought to board, or challenged the English to do so. Instead, Elizabeth's ship came within culverin range, poured in a broadsides, sailed on, and the next English vessel did the same, and the next.

On Wednesday, 3 August, the fighting began early, increased fiercely then tapered off. The same on Thursday, but with losses beginning to mount. On Friday with powder and shot running dangerously short on both sides, the English at least had the advantage of a friendly coast close by; the Spaniards had no source nearer than Portugal to replenish them.

They had been in the Channel a week, had sustained losses in men and ships, were heading into the treacherous North Sea, and so far Parma had not come out—for an excellent reason—he was not prepared to leave shore, for although he had certainly had enough time to create his fleet of barges, it had not been done. Not adequately anyway.

The battle continued on Sunday. On Monday, 8 August, Parma finally left Bruges bound for his camp. On Tuesday the ninth and Wednesday the tenth he ordered the barges to be readied, and by the tenth it was too late; Philip's Armada was running before the wind, its bristling defensive formation broken by fire-ships as well as by deadly nimble English gunships.

At Gravelines the Spaniards fought England and the weather, were battered by both, and in a savage rain-squall swung loose to avoid more collisions, and later, when they limped raggedly about to offer fresh combat, the English declined. The battle was over, the Armada was smashed, Parma was still upon the wrong side of the Channel, King Philip's years-long planning—and prodigious expense—were for nought. Elizabeth was so relieved she went walking among her subjects sharing tears with them, and from the Intelligence standpoint, what historians were to have field-days with ever after, should never have happened at all.

4

After Sir Francis

During those stirring months prior to the sailing of Philip's Armada when England's seagoing highwaymen raked Spain's coasts, and when Drake with thirty ships struck at the humpbacked promontory where Cadiz stood above its magnificent harbour, there had been little discernible strategy, simply a freebooter's tactics which consisted of surprise, noise, plunder, gunsmoke, terror and confusion.

At the same time, in 1587 at Lisbon, a similar attack with greater force would almost certainly have ruined Philip's hopes altogether. Instead Cadiz was raided. Later, in the spring of 1588 when Drake eventually thought of raiding Lisbon Harbour, the place bristled with shore batteries, there were vigilant squadrons watching and waiting, and Drake's chances for success would have been slight.

His proposal was simple. He would blockade Lisbon Harbour with fifty war vessels, and in the event the Spaniards came forth to fight he would destroy them. Intelligence reports advised London that the Spaniards had one hundred warships lying in wait. Concerning Drake's proposal undoubtedly there were Englishmen whose reaction was the same as Philip's had been to other and similar schemes. *Disparo!* Nonsense!

However there was one alternative course, one which in later times would not have been overlooked. And although no one advocated it in 1588 there was reason to believe it would have captured the heart of Queen Elizabeth, because its cost would have been negligible.

Lisbon had a squadron of warships patrolling its sea-lane approaches. It had sentinels aloft by day and by night watching for English sails. It had great guns dowelled into place among shoreline fortifications which commanded every yard of water for miles out to sea.

Despite Francis Drake's confidence during the construction of *La*

Invencible Armada no enemy could have arrived undetected. Between the de Rocca and Setúbal headlands a constant vigil was maintained over every approach to Lisbon Harbour.

No one could have arrived as had Drake at Cadiz, but even had it been possible fifty English ships manned by mariners as valorous and stubborn as only Englishmen could be, would not have been able to enter the harbour, and the chances were excellent that most would never again have seen England.

Where then had Walsingham and others erred? On the landward side.

All roads leading to Lisbon were choked with supply caravans. Hordes of Spaniards, Portuguese, Italians and French moved through clouds of dust behind thousands of burdened beasts. Every night multitudes sank down beside hundreds of campfires, exhausted, clamorous, disorganized because of the stupendous effort required to sustain the greatest accumulation of warships to be assembled in Europe up to that time.

While every sentry was watching seaward and thousands of babbling and alien caravaneers crowded and jostled in the harbour's narrow roadways, Elizabeth's spy-master missed the opportunity of a lifetime by neglecting to infiltrate a mere two hundred demolition-terrorists capable of rowing—and swimming—out to attach explosives under the bows and sterns of Philip's warships. *The Great Armada could have been destroyed at anchor.*

It did not happen, and those who in retrospect defensively suggest that it is easy some four centuries later to see what should have been done, should also appreciate that then as now, the exclusive reason for an Intelligence function was not only to detect peril, but also to explore *all avenues* for negating it.

Another case which could be advanced in extenuation might be based upon an assumption that in Elizabeth's era the English Intelligence systems lacked a 'bureau of dirty tricks'.

As a matter of fact they *did* include such departments, and upon a number of occasions Sir Francis Walsingham sent forth individuals as well as squads whose assignments included overt violence. Rarely throughout history have Intelligence operations been exclusively confined to the accumulation of information, regardless of contrary assertions.

Walsingham in particular was a man of risk, violence, action and intrigue, and it is a fact that at his instigation not all the assassins sent out by Philip of Spain to murder Elizabeth of England reached gaol.

A more plausible clue to Walsingham's oversight emerges after an examination in depth of other factors. After the Armada's departure from the Channel an Englishman wrote to Walsingham that "your honour may see how our parsimony at home hath bereaved us of the famousest victory that ever our navy might have had at sea" and Sir Francis responded in equal gloom: "So our half-doing doth breed dishonour and leaves the disease uncured". This leaves an impression that Walsingham, unhappy over how the matter of the Armada was handled, would certainly have at least attempted to destroy Philip's fleet at anchor *had such an idea occurred to him.*

Why did such an obvious solution not occur to Walsingham in the span of several years during which he was involved with that monumental peril?

Walsingham was an ailing man before the Armada sailed. He only survived its appearance in the Channel by barely two years. In 1587 when Mary, Queen of Scots was executed he was frequently unable to leave his bed. By 1588 his health had noticeably deteriorated. He had not been able to function at peak capacity since about 1585, and during the crucial year when the Armada left Lisbon bound for England, Francis Walsingham had become one of those individuals whose external commitments were increasingly subject to the vicissitudes of his personal physical problems.

In the end Walsingham's oversight abetted history. The Armada's arrival off England provided Queen Elizabeth with reason to make a number of her most ringing pronouncements. His oversight also demonstrated both sides of the Intelligence issue—success and failure—aspects of a unique duality which according to the available records have always existed in English—in all—secret services.

There have been innumerable instances when *sub rosa* interludes have been so bizarre that it has been almost impossible to separate success from failure, a condition which has often arisen from the inability of history to make a judgment until decades, even generations, afterwards.

Sixty years after the demise of Mary, Queen of Scots, for example, her grandson King Charles I did not turn out a single state paper coded or otherwise which was not read and copied by a

clergyman named James Wallis, one of England's foremost cryptanalysts, described in the words of a contemporary as "a person of
reall worth" who "may stand very gloriously upon his own basis,
and need not be beholding to any man of Fame, yet he is so
extremely greedy of glorie, that he steales feathers from others to
adorn his own cap".

Wallis was a brilliant mathematician. Within three months he
broke a code others had been struggling with for two years, and as
cryptanalyst to the Parliamentarians during England's Civil War,
Wallis was able to break the king's codes and thus reveal monarchist
plans so that the Parliamentarians could defeat His Majesty with
such resounding success that Charles followed his grandmother to
the block in 1649 enabling the Puritan party to rule England for the
ensuing eleven years.

Wallis's talent materially abetted the downfall of a monarchy. It
would remain for historians to argue whether that was a failure for
England, or a success. They can still argue it.

Honours accrued to John Wallis, and he unrelentingly sought
them. He became a high Church official and when in 1660 Charles II
became King of England the man who had been largely instrumental in bringing his father to the block, John Wallis, became His
Majesty's spy-master and eventually also his chaplain.

Wallis also became well off. He charged a fee for his cryptanalytical work and the more indispensable he became the higher
his fee became.

Along with being the forerunner of England's outstanding code-
breakers John Wallis was also a notable bureaucrat. He brought his
grandson William Blencowe into the Intelligence organization and
managed to have the government pay for young Blencowe's
tutelage.

In 1703 John Wallis died, a man whose passing was little noted
and whose formidable presence while alive unquestionably
advanced the causes he served with infinitely more success than
most of the generals, statesmen and admirals whose names adorn all
the pages of English history of his era.

His grandson, William Blencowe, became the first English
Intelligence chief to be officially entitled 'Decypherer', and to be
employed on an annual basis with a regular salary, and while he was
talented, William Blencowe committed suicide—or so official
records attest—in 1712 after nine years in the position of His

Majesty's Decypherer, at the age of twenty-nine.

If it was not suicide, and that possibility strongly existed, then His Majesty's Decypherer William Blencowe became the first official spy-master in modern English history to be murdered.

By the year 1712 England's Intelligence community had ceased to be defensive. There were no new invincible armadas on the horizon and although English spies were under sound cover in such congenitally troublesome places as Ireland, Wales and Scotland, domestic dissent while always alive and occasionally also healthy seemed to be subjugated by the compelling necessity among the majority of Britons to eke out an existence before the advent of the Industrial Revolution when cottage commerce and a hidebound agrarianism left little room for pastimes not connected with personal and immediate survival.

But the winds of great change were beginning to blow and while they had little to do with domestic difficulties, the English adaptation of an earlier axiom—divide and conquer—which became a foreign policy based upon preventing continental alliances among hostile powers which would enable enemies to have more sea and land power than England had, put the English espionage capability upon a fresh tangent. Intelligence agents were assigned to every major European capital. They were also sent to all overseas colonies. Friendly, as well as unfriendly and potentially hostile, nations became Intelligence targets. The Secret Intelligence Service (S.I.S) was in many ways more advanced than were the armed services which employed it, or which benefited from its employment by the central government, but in 1756 when England's involvement in the Seven Years War resulted in a major test of the Intelligence function, His Majesty's Decypherer had become only one part of a system whose purpose was to break codes, of course, but which was also to accumulate vast amounts of information along with being able to influence foreign policies and politics.

By that time Edward Willes was England's spy-master and like James Wallis, Willes was a clergyman. Also like Wallis, Edward Willes was a very ambitious individual. By the year 1742 when Willes had received appointment as Bishop of Bath and Wells, his son was official decypherer, and in fact the Willes family represented England's increasingly sophisticated Intelligence community for the ensuing three generations, or until after the turn of the nineteenth century.

During their tenure the title 'His Majesty's Decypherer' was altered to fit the times. All cryptanalysts were lumped together as members of the Decyphering Branch, which was part of the Secret Office. Another facility, the Private Office, had authority for internal espionage including censoring domestic mail. It was in effect a forerunner of M.I.5. Its concerns were primarily with espionage, infiltration, and counter-espionage in Britain.

The Secret Office was charged with reading foreign mail, diplomatic dispatches, and as much of the personal journals and diaries of foreign diplomats in England as it could get its hands on. In this respect it was an earlier version of D.I.5 which was the proper designation of M.I.5 after subordination of armed service S.I.S systems to the Ministry of Defence.

In later times there would have been cries of outrage over the assumption that with the establishment of the postal service in 1657, England's internal security bureaux would be able to read the mail of anyone they chose. Subsequent laws confirmed this privilege.

In defence of the need for this prerogative there was the case of Edward Willes's successful uncovering of a plot by the Bishop of Rochester, Francis Atterbury, to create an uprising against King George I and replace him with a pretender.

Out of this case, which was heard in the House of Lords, George I who was ignorant of both the language and customs of England, emerged unscathed—as well as unloved—while at the same time as a result of Atterbury's persistent attacks upon Willes's espionage credibility, there emerged a famous precedent. After censuring the plotter-priest, the Lords voted that "it is not consistent with the public Safety to ask the Decypherers any Questions which may tend to discover the Art or Mystery of Decyphering".

Bishop Atterbury was convicted and banished from England, and although subsequently he was all but lost to history, that act of the Lords in defence of secrecy paved the way in the seventeenth century for the ultimate adoption of England's Official Secrets Act which provided penalties for the disclosure of specific restricted information, and prosecution under this act could be inaugurated without disclosure of the restricted material. Through the 'D Notice' system, English publishers were invited to voluntarily abstain from making public anything which would compromise military secrets, or which might endanger national security. Because the Official Secrets Act was entirely enforceable there were few deliberate violations.

What had been occurring with consistent regularity throughout the English Intelligence community since Francis Walsingham's day was a steadily improving espionage capability. For a long while after the establishment of both the Private Office and the Secret Office no more than a handful of people knew these bureaux existed. Fewer people had knowledge of how professionally expert England's secret services had become. Spies of considerable ability sent encoded reports to the deciphering rooms ('Black Chambers') from every critical area of the world. After the middle of the eighteenth century when England's North American colonies became troublesome, spies more than royal governors or loyal soldiers provided London with the kinds of information which enabled King George III and his cabinet officials to appreciate well in advance of a general understanding, that colonial sentiment was tending towards armed confrontation, even though most Englishmen did not believe this and a number of influential Americans were equally unconvinced.

5

The Thicket

With the exception of the Second World War it is quite possible that no political upheaval England ever became involved in had such a vast and bewildering array of spies as the American Rebellion, and uniquely the one individual most noted for defection, espionage and treachery, Benedict Arnold, was the least productive of the secret agents serving England.

For over two centuries Arnold has been vilified for what he *might* have done, not for what he actually achieved, because in actuality he accomplished nothing as an English secret agent although he clearly hoped to materially advance England's designs in the New World and wrote to that affect with typical lack of discretion.

Generally, however, England's spy-masters profited greatly from their association with dissident Americans. Before the rebellion had run its course they had been literally overwhelmed by secret offers of collaboration from Americans of every class and position.

Also, while English commanders in the New World sought dutifully to recruit dissident rebels they had their own Intelligence cadres, but their best source of Intelligence throughout was the Americans themselves, primarily one may assume because independence and actual separation were by no means unanimously desired. Confirmed Tories, colonial loyalists, and simply sympathetic colonists who were certain all the difficulties could be amicably settled through conciliatory negotiation, when war came, chose to oppose the radical fire-brands such as Patrick Henry, John Adams, and Thomas Paine, none of whom initially spoke for an American majority.

It was to a considerable extent these settled colonists who served as spies, demolitionists, infiltrators and assassins for His Majesty George III—called by many Americans 'Farmer George'.

At home, the Secret Office with its responsibility for spying on aliens in Britain, and the Private Office busier than ever censoring domestic mail, had their hands full because this conflict, which was more nearly a civil war than a revolution, was not popular among the British either, and dissent was widespread. So widespread that during the earlier stages at Westminster a representative leapt to his feet and said, "I warn the ministers that if they persist in their wretched course of oppression, the whole continent of North America will rise up in arms and the colonies perhaps be lost forever to England."

Letters leaving England which were discreetly opened and read rarely approved the Crown's course, while those entering the country from the Continent, and elsewhere, were in general equally unfavourable. Documents from German, French and Spanish diplomatic pouches hinted early on that now was probably an excellent time for Albion's traditional enemies to form an alliance against her.

What the Intelligence offices verified was nothing the public did not already realize. Dissatisfaction was not only widespread it was also vociferous. Nor did the secret reports offer any surprises to His Majesty. He knew very well despite the toadying denials of Germain, North and others, that Crown policy was dividing England, was injurious to national prestige, and was setting two-thirds of the Continent against Britain. But George III, while possessed of diligence, administrative ability and strength of character, also, as Trevelyan has noted "had not imagination".

While at home the drum was beaten and the king's coin was an added inducement, recruits came, but never in adequate quantities nor very willingly, so Germans had eventually to be hired to wage George's war, and overseas the incredible confusion in America steadily increased, not entirely in the Intelligence sector but elsewhere as well. For example hundreds of loyal refugees poured into British-held Boston in 1775, and according to official records 1,124 more straggled after General Howe when he marched for Halifax in the spring of 1776, and slightly more than a year later 3,111 loyal Americans marched beside the redcoats to New York. So many Americans flocked to the king's side that not only were entire armed units made up of them, but secret agents recruited from these same multitudes roamed behind colonial lines by the hundreds, right up to the fateful calamity at Yorktown, sending reams of secret intelligence.

The need for imported specialists from England, while envisioned as an early necessity by the armed forces Intelligence sector, in fact never existed. If technical logistical information was required English gold could buy American experts. Defectors were everywhere. On 28 June 1776 one Thomas Hickey was condemned and hanged in a field "near the Bowery Lane", in New York City "in the presence of near 20,000 spectators" for "treacherously corresponding with, enlisting among, and receiving pay from the enemies of the United American Colonies".

Thomas Hickey was a member of George Washington's personal guard.

At best Hickey had been marginally valuable. In the same year British Commander-in-Chief Sir Henry Clinton did much better. He secured the services as secret agent of Metcalf Bowler, former speaker of the Rhode Island Assembly, Chief Justice, and successful merchant of Newport.

Few Americans had such access to rebel high councils as did Justice Bowler. No American would question the patriotism of a man who had been one of the signers of his state's Declaration of Independence. Yet his patriotism lasted exactly four days after Clinton took Rhode Island as a base for the New England campaign.

Having "been unwarily led from my duty to the King", he told General Clinton, "and having joined the provincials in their opposition to his Majesty's government" he now sought reinstatement as a loyal subject and to prove his sincerity volunteered to spy for Sir Henry, "though should it ever come to the knowledge of the provincials, shall run a violent risk of my life".

He did in fact successfully spy for General Clinton and as with hundreds like him Metcalf Bowler's incentive arose from a personal conviction that the Americans could not win their insurrection. (Ironically, Sir Henry Clinton was equally certain that they could not lose it.)

Sir Henry, as commander in America, had an endless series of details to oversee. It did not help that his route of supply was as wide as the Atlantic Ocean. Neither did it help that obesity plagued him, that the Americans mercilessly harassed him, and that he had a terrible disposition, refusing for days at a time to talk to anyone.

He took no delight at all in espionage and although he was perfectly aware of the necessity for it he delegated responsibility to subordinates, most of whom, quite fortunately, were dedicated and adept.

Eventually he was to acquire a sprightly, rather unprincipled young opportunist, Major John André, who would supervise—and become the principal victim of—the most notorious Intelligence plot of the rebellion, the Arnold affair. André was also eventually to epitomize the tragic circumstances of captured spies in wartime —and to also illustrate the foolishness of carrying incriminating documents in one's boots. However, prior to André's advent Sir Henry Clinton acquired a colonial named James Hammill, an Irishman who was serving as an American major, and aide to the Continental commanding officer of two Hudson River forts which the British captured in the autumn of 1777. Hammill volunteered to defect and Sir Henry accepted the offer.

Hammill was secretly delivered behind American lines, but before he had accomplished much an anonymous letter to American authorities accusing him of espionage for the enemy resulted in his apprehension.

He escaped from custody after a court martial had sentenced him to the gallows. He was never reinstated by British Intelligence, lived out the war in dire need among the loyalists, and eventually died a few years after the war in abject poverty.

Not all defectors produced dazzling results, obviously, nor retired weighted down with honours, but then not many American turncoats were men of the stature of Chief Justice Bowler or 'the fightingest general of the Rebellion', Benedict Arnold. For all the top-level information sent in by these high dignitaries it was actually dissidents in the ranks, in the towns and villages who supplied royal authorities with the greatest bulk of their secret intelligence.

And along with the spies there were also many avowed loyalists whose familiarity with customs, terrain and the inevitable waverers, enabled them to blow up bridges, establish ambuscades, procure information through torture, burn rebel supplies and sow virulent discontent. The number of colonials willing to defect increased proportionately to British military successes, and decreased according to British defeats, but among loyalists who had never served the cause of rebellion, there was from beginning to end very little defection. Almost none at all in fact. These people were highly successful infiltrators and spies with special capabilities which they were encouraged to develop by British Intelligence and so great was their success that almost no American corps, assembly, council or command was not infiltrated by spies who were native Americans.

So serious did this condition become that Congress itself got into the business of examining suspects through a committee chaired by John Jay, a representative from New York, and eventual President of the Continental Congress.

Jay had the distinction of uncovering an espionage and recruitment ring in his native New York City headed by David Mathews, the mayor, while another New Yorker, Herman Zedwitz, a colonel in the 1st New York Regiment of the continental army, formerly in British service, not only volunteered to spy for the British by sending them an "Acurat State of the Armee", every week in exchange for remuneration in the amount of £4,000 payable in advance, but also as an inducement darkly confided that the Americans were going to poison "a watering place".

Zedwitz proved to be that phenomenon of the espionage vocation, an individual who was not filtered out before it was discovered that he was a somewhat odd character. But for every Herman Zedwitz there were dozens like Major William Demont, adjutant to Colonel Robert Magaw of the 5th Pennsylvania regiment, who was not exposed by John Jay's Congressional Committee, nor any other investigative body, in time.

Demont was part of the durable garrison at Fort Washington, the last rebel stronghold on Manhattan after the British had driven the main American army north to White Plains and beyond.

In order for British control to be complete, and also because it would be intolerable to have several thousand rebels in a fort in their midst, British commanders considered means for reducing Colonel Magaw's stronghold.

Any attack would have to cross over open ground in the face of what Intelligence reports indicated would be at least 2,500 well-armed and provisional defenders, and there was no enthusiasm at all for that kind of assault.

That was the situation before Demont, the 'walk-in' slipped out of Fort Washington at night, got safely to the British lines and was escorted to the commander where he unfolded a map of Fort Washington's interior, which was interesting but not invaluable, then also drew a diagram of how the British, by taking advantage of obstacles and oversights, might successfully capture Fort Washington at negligible cost. The results were noted in official reports: Fort Washington "was taken by his Majesty's troops the 16th instant

[November] together with 2700 prisoners, and stores of ammunition to the amount of £1800".

Not inaccurately William Demont said of his betrayal, "I may
with justice affirm, from my knowledge of the works, I saved the
lives of many of his Majesty's subjects," but at least one American
of the garrison, Captain Alexander Graydon, with ample time to
reflect while in captivity, was of the opinion that the successful
British assault had to have been devised by someone who "must
have had perfect knowledge of the ground".

It was this variety of espionage, defection and betrayal which
made the importation of orthodox secret agents unnecessary. Nor
was the Fort Washington episode unique. Among the dozens of
similar successful betrayals by other 'walk-ins', were at least two
secret offers by Americans to sell the most strategic fortification on
the invasion route from Canada, Fort Ticonderoga, and the last
time the offer was made, the initiator offered as an additional
inducement to throw in General Washington.

This instigator's name was Benedict Arnold and although his
perfidy was complete with all the signs, countersigns, clandestine
rendezvous, assumed names, furtive signals, codes and secret intermediaries, it was a dismal failure. General Arnold's coded message
informing the British when Washington could be captured was
as follows:

120.9.14.286.9.33-ton 290.9127. be at 153.9.28. 110.8.19.255.9.29
evening 148.8.8 on 131.9.34. 287.8.33 to 128.9.24.144.9.10.286.5.16.
he is to. 167.9.27 thru 116.9.23.12.19.7. and 120.9.11. and 290.9.27.
160.9.123. at 190. o.32.153.9.20.

This was translated by General Clinton's intermediary, Jonathon
Odell, as: "General Washington will be at Kings Ferry Sunday
evening next on his way to Hartford where he is to meet the French
Admiral and General. And will lodge at Peekskill."

The abrupt denouement of Arnold's plans saved Washington
from an abduction which might, as has been claimed, have ended
the Rebellion, though that seems doubtful now. At the very least a
successful abduction would have had considerable influence on
further rebel policy. More, one may conjecture, than the selling of
Fort Ticonderoga, which already had a chequered past having been
owned at one time or another by just about everyone marching
either south into the Colonies or North into Canada. Although it
was strategically placed, it had had only a slight effect on basic

events north or south, regardless of what ensign flew from the flagstaff.

Another American of substance who served the Crown, this time in a number of exalted positions not the least of which was spy-master, was William Franklin, the son of the renowned American Benjamin Franklin. At one time the younger Franklin served at Fort Ticonderoga as twenty-year-old captain of His Majesty's army.

He was never a rebel and in 1762 was appointed Royal Governor of New Jersey. Subsequently, in direct opposition to his famous father and having denounced rebels as traitors and worse, he was declared an enemy of the Revolution and was placed under house arrest by the Americans. He was eventually paroled, but his out-spoken denigration resulted in re-arrest and this time he was imprisoned for seeking to re-assemble a loyal legislative assembly which had been abolished by the Americans.

At one time young Franklin served as General Clinton's com-missioner of Intelligence. He performed very well, organized espionage cells behind American lines, created clandestine groups whose purpose was to disrupt transport, supply and communication facilities, and he also sent forth assassination teams. It was his involvement in the hanging of an American soldier, Captain Joshua Huddy, which even General Clinton called plain murder, that pre-cipitated such a violent reaction even among fellow loyalists, that young Franklin's career in America was irredeemably damaged.

Captain Huddy had been captured in battle. By existing codes he was entitled to honourable incarceration, and believed he was to get it, when Franklin's men removed him from a stockade by telling him there was to be a routine interrogation. Instead they tied his arms behind his back and hanged him from a tree where Americans would find the body and be intimidated.

Something to the contrary occurred. Such violent reaction occurred that Sir Henry Clinton feared British prisoners in American hands would be hanged in retaliation. General Washing-ton, normally a circumspect individual, angrily threatened bloody retaliation over what he, and a great many of the British, termed an affair of cold-blooded murder.

William Franklin sailed for England where he was given a grant of £1,800 and was later accorded a lifetime pension of £800.

He died in 1813, surviving his famous father by twenty-three years. He and his father, whose politics had been so different for so long, managed in 1784 to affect a semblance of an ending of their long estrangement, four years before the elder Franklin died, but Benjamin's feeling of reconciliation was not sufficiently strong to include an inheritance of any kind for his Tory son.

As the Rebellion neared its climax the flood of Intelligence tended to verify what history had been demonstrating since earliest times: when an idea's time has come, neither the grandest armies nor the most sophisticated Intelligence system under the sun can do more than delay some variety of inevitable change. Those who were unaware of this, normally followed the course of men such as British under-secretary William Eden—later Lord Aukland—whose refusal to believe the British defeat at Saratoga seriously impaired England's hegemony overseas and resulted in an endless series of pointless little intrigues.

It also resulted in an economic drain. Before Yorktown, between 1 January and 26 May 1777 the approximate pound sterling equivalent of $13,000 was paid by Sir Henry Clinton for secret service purposes—spying, rewards and incentives—a fortune in those times, and that, for less than half a year.

Where England's spies and turncoats of the Rebellion had difficulty was less with the rule of pay than it was with other emoluments they felt were due them such as pensions, academic and political appointments, decorations and honours.

Generally the government was sympathetic, but fundamentally the perfidy of many Americans who had spied for England against their fellow colonials, left them vulnerable to the disdain of people of ethics on both sides of the Atlantic.

The result was that while His Majesty's government lived up to most of its verifiable commitments, once the conflict ended, the clear tendency was to allow wartime undertakings simply to die a natural death.

But in the Intelligence communities different rules have traditionally applied. Military defeats even catastrophic, final ones have seldom resulted in an end to the secret campaigns. In many instances quite to the contrary; military débâcles have caused a redoubling of clandestine efforts. And without exception the secret services have been most active during peace negotiations.

History abounds with examples of secret manipulations among negotiators during periods of transition at the conclusion of conflicts, which have resulted in coups armies and navies were unable to achieve, and these meetings have commonly demonstrated that diplomacy is nothing more nor less than the respectable face of the Intelligence function. Negotiators have rarely sat down to bargain without having first been briefed by the Intelligence sector.

England's spy-masters were some of the most accomplished in the world. When it was announced that peace negotiations between His Majesty's commissioners and their American counterparts were by common consent scheduled to take place in Paris, the men whose access to the bureaux of power were by the backstairs, were satisfied.

Paris, foremost city of a nation more often hostile to England than any other country, had a seasoned, firmly established British Intelligence cadre already in place. That, as well as the ability and expertise of the moles of Whitehall, augured well for those whose professional purpose and personal desire was to manipulate both the king's negotiators and the American peace commissioners so that it might be possible to salvage a few of the chestnuts Burgoyne, the Howe brothers, Clinton and Cornwallis had lost in the New World.

6

The Backstairs of Paris

A number of attempts at conciliation were made by His Majesty's government beginning shortly after the first gunshots were exchanged, and continuing right up to the time of John Burgoyne's defeat at Saratoga, the first major armed triumph of the rebel cause.

The Colonial Congress had several representatives in Paris when news of Burgoyne's defeat reached the Continent. Their purpose was, if possible, to promote an alliance between France, England's ancient antagonist, and England's rebelling North American colonies.

These American treaty commissioners became the target of a discreet series of secret service schemes, but before they were to be approached it was decided that an assessment had to first be made respecting the French reaction to Burgoyne's defeat.

At that time, autumn 1777, the British Intelligence service on the Continent was adroitly managed by William Eden, whose personal views after the defeat at Saratoga encouraged him to strive harder than ever to prevent disunion.

His private conviction that even if the Americans achieved independence, because of their relative weakness they must inevitably fall under some form of European control, encouraged him not illogically to say that according to customs, language and heritage, the North Americans would be better off as Britons, even under easier terms than previously offered through the Crown's earlier conciliation efforts.

It was this proposal the government wanted conveyed to the American representatives in Paris after Saratoga. The Crown could not, it seemed, deal openly with the rebels in Paris, but through spymaster Eden it was willing to seriously consider any American suggestions, except one: independence.

This approach seemed harmless enough, but the secret agent

selected to convey it was anything but harmless although the Americans in Paris did not realize it.

His name was Paul Wentworth. His American credentials were excellent. He was a former member of the New Hampshire Council, and had been in London for some time as an American spy. He had become a double agent through an agreement with the second Earl of Guilford, Lord North, then Prime Minister, a man fully cognizant of the value of secret services.

Wentworth, who received £200 annually as a British spy, although American born, was something of a cosmopolitan. He travelled extensively on the Continent, did business as an entrepreneur in the Lowlands as well as in London and Paris, lived well and had flourished as a businessman since his arrival in England.

How much he actually ferreted out for the Americans is open to conjecture, although he must have satisfied them to some extent otherwise it seems improbable that they would not have recalled him.

His personal desires were no secret. He coveted a baronetcy, some form of respected political appointment, acceptance into the very stratified British society of those times, and a life of comfort.

He owned land in New Hampshire and because he expected eventually to renounce his ties with the rebels, he had to be re-assured by the English his lands would remain inviolate.

Paul Wentworth was not especially unique as a spy. He was certain the Crown would triumph in America, and aside from a personal preference for civilized England, he had his private interests at heart.

He was a good spy, although he scorned other spies and did not want to be known as a spy. He preferred to delude himself with the idea that he was a diplomat, and to some degree in his dealing with the Americans in Paris he functioned as one. In this assumed role of negotiator for the Crown he made a number of pronouncements, one of which was interestingly revealing. In America, he said, corruption was rampant at all levels. He was convinced that most rebel Americans were motivated by greed, self-interest, envy and ambition. "A well-timed offer of indemnity", he wrote, "and impunity to these Cromwells and Barebones may serve us like a strong alkali."

Wentworth particularly disliked one of the American commis-sioners, Benjamin Franklin of Pennsylvania. The other two, Silas

Deane of Connecticut and Arthur Lee of Virginia, were known to him—and to Eden's Intelligence organization—only as Americans who had been affiliated with rebel councils since the Rebellion's earliest days. Franklin however, had always been an outspoken correspondent. He still was in late 1777, but earlier the Secret Office had monitored a letter of Franklin's which said in part that "if America would save for three or four years the money she spends in fashion and fineries and fopperies of this country [England], she might buy the whole Parliament, ministers and all", and that particular comment had done absolutely nothing to endear Franklin to Eden, Wentworth, or a great many other sensitive Britons. In fact, King George considered Benjamin Franklin the arch-rebel of them all.

Of course for several years now Britain had been buying Americans in almost wholesale lots. Benjamin Franklin's personal secretary was a British spy. James Vardill of New York, another native American in London, diligently spied on other Americans in Europe and Britain for His Majesty's secret service. It was commonly thought among British officials that Congress itself would be corruptible if some way could be devised to approach it.

This being the prevailing view, it was thought that Franklin, Deane, or Arthur Lee could be corrupted in Paris, and Wentworth's secret instructions without a doubt were to attempt such a subornation.

Edward Bancroft of Massachusetts, Franklin's confidant, had been a British spy even before sailing with Franklin for Paris. His assignment in France was to watch the commissioners, co-operate with other English spies who might appear, and to report every act of Franklin, Deane and Lee to Eden's secret service.

Clearly, however, this avenue of clandestine intrigue was of uncertain promise, because when Paul Wentworth appeared in Paris, Doctor Franklin refused even to meet him unless it were first clearly understood that under no circumstances "in any part of the conversation" was the topic of collusion to be mentioned.

Even then, when assurances had been given, the two men did not meet until January 1778, almost a month after Wentworth's arrival in France.

Wentworth had a letter, written by Eden, to show Franklin in which it was stated that England was prepared to continue the war for ten years if necessary to prevent independence. Franklin's answer was that the Americans would, if necessary, fight fifty years to gain independence.

Wentworth did not give up easily, but his best efforts were at length unavailing. Franklin said calmly that separation was mutually advantageous; that such a fact was not even arguable, but that he also believed Britain and America should be bound together by trade.

Wentworth reported to Eden, and meanwhile, unbeknown to Wentworth his arrival in Paris had accelerated the very thing England wished to prevent. Fearful that America's commissioners might be prevailed upon, either through persuasion or bribery, to reach an accord with the British, the French told Franklin, Deane and Lee that the king's council had decided to recognize American independence, which meant the way was formally open for an alliance between France and the rebellious English colonies.

Wentworth's presence in Paris, a secret agent for England's monarch, was used by the French Foreign Minister, Compte de Vergennes, as an argument with Spain's ambassador to the French king's court to promote a tripartite treaty; France, Spain and America, against Britain.

Vergennes wrote that "The power which first recognizes the independence of the Americas will be the first one to gather all the fruits of this war."

Spain was cautious. Without refusing to join France and the Americans, the Spanish king preferred a course of procrastination until he could delve more deeply into the affair and meanwhile Paul Wentworth received a reply to his report on Doctor Franklin's intransigence: approach the other two envoys, Lee of Virginia and Deane of Connecticut.

Perhaps Wentworth had already appraised Arthur Lee of Virginia. He almost certainly had met him by this stage of Eden's scheme, so it is possible that he knew Lee had a violent temper, a sharp tongue and would use both if he were riled.

On the other hand Lee had made no secret of a cynical conviction that most men could be bought, a sentiment Paul Wentworth shared. But in any event Wentworth's brief encounter with the Virginian convinced him Lee was not to be corrupted, so Wentworth moved along to the one remaining commissioner, Silas Deane.

Here, Wentworth's diplomatic language seemed to reach a

sympathetic ear. Deane, said Eden's agent, could have "the honour of pointing out the mode and means of salvation to his country" and the "dignity and emoluments" this would bring him would derive from a grateful English king.

Silas Deane was a crafty, inward man, cautious under most circumstances. He listened and said nothing at this particular meeting with Wentworth, the fellow-American, but at a subsequent meeting he evinced careful interest in what exactly those emoluments entailed. Wentworth, following instructions based upon what Eden's secret service knew of Americans in this respect, reported that His Majesty would offer "honours and emoluments to the leaders, governors, generals, privy seals, great seals, treasurers, secretaries, councilers in the general government, local barons, and knights", in American, if the Crown triumphed, the rebellion were put down, and Britain's system of government and social order were re-established.

Silas Deane was a discreet individual. Nothing as indicative of perfidy was left behind by him as it was with Benedict Arnold. Nor were secret service records available even after Deane's death in 1789 to indicate the extent, or even the actual existence of treachery and deceit.

But he was engaging in commercial ventures while in Paris as a treaty commissioner, and there were signs that he had affected some kind of arrangement with someone in London to be provided with advance information on commodities, which enabled him to profit comfortably.

Paul Wentworth returned to London for a conference with his spy-master, William Eden, in early January, and near the end of the month Lord North notified His Majesty that a number of purchases had been authorized of trade goods by Paul Wentworth, to be shipped to New York to the care of a 'Mr D'. Along with this, Lord North also wrote to King George that herewith are "Mr D's proposals, to which are added some pieces of intelligence Mr W. received from him". These were in the nature of secret disclosures.

'Mr D' was certainly Silas Deane. 'Mr W' was equally certainly Paul Wentworth, but what those "proposals" were Mr D offered, remain a secret to this day.

However, during the course of Deane's association with the spy Wentworth he had used the name 'Benson' upon several occasions, and finally His Majesty wrote to Lord North that "if the intelligence sent by Benson is founded, France has taken her part and a war with Great Britain must soon follow", the implication being that 'Benson' Deane had procured an early copy of the French-American accords for Wentworth to take back to London with him.

King George was not pleased at the news Eden sent him through Lord North, but he was clearly impressed with Wentworth's success at suborning one of Congress' special envoys.

It was to be a short-lived sense of accomplishment however, because Deane was recalled by Congress and at this time doughty John Adams was assigned in his place. If there was any concern over Deane's recall it evidently did not extend to King George who, upon hearing that Deane was to return to Philadelphia, thought it a "very fortunate event", and one he hoped would, along with his government's latest conciliation offer, help to bring "America [back] to a state of tranquillity".

The conciliation project, however, and despite the fact that it was eventually literally carried to Philadelphia by English envoys —one of which was spy-master William Eden—came to nothing. Saratoga had been followed by additional rebel triumphs in arms, none approaching the magnitude of Burgoyne's defeat but all together sufficiently impressive to stiffen rebel resolve, now that France and also Spain were American allies.

As for the business of incessant meddling, it was not confined to the English. Benjamin Franklin also tried his hand at conspiracy by secretly sending an American associate, Jonathon Loring Austin, to London for the purpose of seeking sympathetic Whig leaders. But like the conciliation commission which would eventually reach America, Franklin's scheme also produced no tangible results.

Twice in March His Majesty's government sent a recruit of its Intelligence sector to see Doctor Franklin in Paris, this time taking greater pains not to arouse the French, as Wentworth's visit had done, but as a matter of fact the French also possessed a respectable espionage and counter-espionage capability. The American envoys were under constant surveillance.

This English agent was William Pulteney, a sometime politician from Shrewsbury who, for his part in the secret project ahead, assumed the name of Williams.

Pulteney's arrival in Paris was uneventful and he had no difficulty in arranging to meet Doctor Franklin. He found the American to be unassuming and congenial. He also found him to be just as intransigent as Paul Wentworth had found him to be. In response to Pulteney's discreet proposals Franklin said, "When I first had the honour of conversing with you on the subject of peace, I mentioned it as my opinion that every proposition which implied our voluntarily agreeing to return to a dependence on Britain was now impossible."

Franklin, ordinarily a man of tact, remained throughout his meeting with 'Mr Williams' an epitome of amiability, and while the Englishman felt encouraged, when he returned to London to report, his employers who were more experienced at this sort of thing expressed scepticism.

His Majesty in particular was convinced that Franklin's "hatred to this country" made it very unlikely anything worthwhile would come of these clandestine efforts. Yet he was unwilling to abandon them. It was, he said, "proper to keep open the channel of intercourse with this insidious man".

He wanted William Pulteney as one of "the agents employed in this dangerous business" to return and have another meeting with Franklin.

This time Pulteney was provided with a letter by Lord North, and approved by the king, for Benjamin Franklin to endorse as a sign of his good faith. He was also supplied with a duplicate copy of the conciliatory proposals which the official peace commission was shortly to deliver in Philadelphia.

'Mr Williams' returned to Paris and sent a note to Franklin advising that he would "be glad to see Doctor Franklin, whenever it is convenient for the Doctor, at the Hotel Frasiliere, rue Tournon".

Whitehall's scepticism proved correct. Benjamin Franklin's second meeting with Pulteney was disillusioning. He refused to endorse North's letter, and as to the conciliatory proposals, he said in affect that since His Majesty's ministers could not "divest themselves of the idea that the power of Parliament over us is . . . absolute and unlimited" there was no possibility of a reconciliation, nor any need for further discussions between himself and Mr Williams.

But Doctor Franklin made one private concession. At Pulteney's request he agreed not to disclose to the French Pulteney's identity nor his purpose in meeting with Franklin.

The Intelligence effort did not end here although it probably should have. Several additional secret agents became involved with the Americans in Paris including George Johnstone a long-time member of Parliament, where he had defended the rights of Americans to take umbrage over Crown excesses although he was absolutely against disunion, and Sir Robert Eden, brother of the spy-master, who actually served more as a diplomat than a spy although at times the matter of delineation was arguable.

But the idea's time had come, and along with that fact went some impressive combat statistics. For the first time since the advent of hostilities American warships were meeting Britons on the high seas in open combat. It was reported in the House of Commons in February of 1778 that American privateers had taken 733 prizes. By that same year on the high seas there were 115 of these seagoing greyhounds, sleek, very fast and heavily armed. In April, the notorious American John Paul Jones had actually landed in England, at Whitehaven, where he spiked the guns of the fort, set fire to a ship in the harbour, sailed over to Carrickfergus in Northern Ireland, engaged His Majesty's warship *Drake*, forced a capitulation and took his prize to France.

On land, in June the Americans under Washington had defeated the British under Clinton at Monmouth and in July they organized the expedition which was to result in the defeat and surrender of Colonel Henry Hamilton in the north. Meanwhile in the south, Americans reinforced by the newly-arrived French were establishing the groundwork which would ultimately result in the Yorktown disaster for Lord Cornwallis, and this event would in turn create the repercussions which in England would result in the fall of Lord North's ministry.

Calamities piled one upon the other. In the West Indies America's French allies inflicted several resounding defeats upon the British and took a number of Britain's West Indian possessions and the Spanish, America's belated ally, threatened British-owned Malta.

The combined navies of Britain's enemies were overwhelmingly superior, and land forces far outnumbered Crown armies.

Lord North's 'coercive policy' of government was repudiated on 27 February 1782 when the House of Commons voted "against further prosecuting the war in America" and passed a bill (5 March) authorizing the Crown to make peace with the former colonies.

Lord Rockingham succeeded Lord North as Prime Minister and at once peace negotiations were seriously undertaken.

Also, fresh clandestine efforts at ameliorating the situation were inaugurated. The war had been lost. It was now time to see whether or not the peace might be won.

Britain's initial peace commissioner was an adept man by the name of Richard Oswald. American negotiators approved by Congress were Benjamin Franklin, Thomas Jefferson, (who never appeared in Paris where the talks were to be held) Henry Laurens, (in ill health after a lengthy incarceration as a British prisoner and who had no influence on the outcome of the conferences) and crusty John Adams. Another American, John Jay the former President of Congress, would arrive in Paris on 23 June 1782 to assist Franklin.

Rockingham, successor to Lord North, died very suddenly and was in turn succeeded by the Earl of Shelburne who vigorously pressed for the conclusion of the treaties.

The French, fearful the Americans might sign a separate treaty with the British despite earlier American assurances to the contrary, placed secret agents in the hotels where the Americans were lodging. The British, more sanguine about their espionage, already had Doctor Franklin's secretary in their employ, so now they attempted to suborn the French as well.

Before the negotiations convened, Britain had very little to lose which had not already been taken from her by force of arms. Her primary concern therefore was to recover as much as possible through negotiation, and foremost among her worries was the fate and the ownership of Canada.

Benjamin Franklin's secretary secretly informed Whitehall that the Americans, led by Franklin and encouraged by the French, intended to insist upon a complete relinquishment of British claims to Canada.

His Majesty's government moved carefully through several secret agents to convey the idea that under no circumstances would the Crown yield on the point of Canada, however His Majesty's government would, in a spirit of generosity and goodwill, concede to an independent America exclusive fishing rights off Newfoundland, as well as the full length of the North American Atlantic coastlands.

When the first move to draft a preliminary treaty was made, American secret agents in London passed along the Intelligence that on the Canadian question alone His Majesty's government would not be moved.

At about this same time British spies learned that in secret session the other American negotiators had refused to support Franklin's demand on Canada. This information was sent at once to London. What it clearly amounted to was the first triumph for British diplomacy. In 1782 the government could not have retained Canada by force of arms, her alternative if the negotiation had failed, primarily because His Majesty's subjects, lords and commoners, were totally opposed to any additional, or continuous adventurism.

From this point forward, considering what was at stake, the negotiations progressed with uncommon celerity. Richard Oswald was joined by fellow-diplomat Henry Strachey on 28 October and on 1 November the Americans, Franklin, Adams, Jay and Laurens went outside the spirit of the conference by treating directly with the British, although they had been instructed by Congress to act jointly with the French.

By 5 November the negotiators were in accord on a set of articles which were to constitute the preliminary treaty.

These were agreed upon and endorsed by Oswald for the British, Franklin, Adams, Jay and Laurens for the Americans, and later, on 3 September 1783, this treaty became the official accord acceptable to the governments of both nations, without a single alteration.

Its most significant highlights for the Americans included British recognition of American independence, the St Croix River to be the boundary between Maine (U.S.) and Nova Scotia (British) a line (later to be contended) from Lake Superior to the Mississippi River dividing Canada from the United States, and all British armed forces to be evacuated from U.S. territory "with all convenient speed".

The American Congress was to advocate that each state seriously consider restitution of the rights and properties of loyalists, a matter which was only indifferently attended to. During the recent conflict American hatred was most virulent towards, first, loyal Americans who were viewed as traitors, secondly Britain's German mercenaries who were generally brutish and unnecessarily cruel, and lastly the Crown troops.

The French Foreign Minister Compte de Vergennes was annoyed with the Americans for coming to an agreement with the British without consulting his government. He was no doubt unaware that British secret agents had informed His Majesty's negotiators that unless they pressed for an immediate bilateral accord Britain could very possibly lose all of Canada; it was known to the British Intelli-

Sir Francis Walsingham, Elizabeth I's spymaster

Johannes Wallis, S.T.D.
Geometriæ Professor Savilianus Oxoniæ

W. Faithorne delin.   et sculp. 1668.

John Wallis, a mathematician and Church official who deciphered intercepted Royalist documents

gence sector that the French wanted French-speaking Canada, and that they had agreed to support an American claim to western Canada, with force if necessary.

In the end Britain had conceded only one thing she had been unwilling to concede before Cornwallis's defeat: independence.

All the rest of it she had been willing to forgo before any serious discussions took place, and all of it had been used earlier as bait.

What she had salvaged was Canada. Her secret agents had performed very well. Beaten by a coterie of strong enemies, unable to sustain additional armed incursions because of adverse popular sentiment at home, her Intelligence sector had learned which were the vulnerable points of her enemies and these were expertly exploited.

Britain returned St Lucia to the French and Trincomalee to the Dutch, then conceded her right to Minorca and Florida to the Spanish, and in turn recovered all her West Indies possessions except Tobago, retained Gibraltar in the face of fierce Spanish opposition, got the French to leave the Cape of Good Hope, and won the privilege of trading throughout the Dutch West Indies.

The emperor of Austria said that Britain, bereft of her empire was now to become "a second-rate power", and would be one "forever". He had to have been a man of very limited vision to believe any nation which appeared at the conference table with as little to bargain with, and which came away with so much as Britain had, would be a "second-rate power" for long.

7

Towards an Ominous Future

The armies and navies which have been an extension of government since earliest times have not always been the "*last* resort of kings".

Nor have they been limited in size and capability to national defence. Any time the armed forces of a nation have considerably exceeded the requirements of defence it has been both reasonable and customary to assume someone's ambition is showing.

The misuse of power is no doubt the oldest of all crimes. Armies have marched and navies have sailed when strong men have decreed that they must, and clearly, if history has taught nothing else it has certainly provided endless lessons to prove that what is legal is not the same as what is just. The law empowered Philip of Spain to squeeze the last copper coin out of his people in order that he might create an awesome armada. The law empowered George III of Great Britain to create intolerable hardship at home so that in his narrow stubbornness he could wage a ruinous war abroad.

At the councils of admirals and field-marshals all the prospects for grand triumphs have historically been discussed, without a single advocate of justice being present.

The cost of the American War had been exorbitant. It had not been a popular conflict even when the populace out of pure and admirable loyalty had supported King George, but clearly as the war years passed and England's economy suffered increasingly, some change was in prospect.

As with all eras when social and political upheavals appeared to be imminent and governments as well as rulers have turned to their best sources of information, the Tories and Whigs of Britain as well as the king's friends, turned to their Intelligence sources.

The Lord Gordon Riots of 1780 which had a religious taint, erupted into a clamorous uprising which, in London alone, had about fifty thousand vociferous adherents, largely destitute people, whose rampages resulted in considerable loss of property, and eventually, when troops were sent against them, also a loss of human life.

This totally Protestant host early abandoned its pretext of religious intolerance and broke into a number of prisons to free gaoled debtors, and it also attacked residences of officials associated with oppressive government, including those concerned with the levying and collecting of taxes.

Without much doubt the American War had left England's economy in a shambles, had created unbearable hardship for the classes of people which could stand it the least, had undermined foreign trade and had greatly inhibited domestic commerce. However even as the American empire was halved with the best port being lost, and while all the doomsday pronouncements were ringing loudest, recovery was under way.

British agents abroad reported that the nation's recent enemies of substance, France and Spain, had become mired in their own difficulties. It was therefore reasonable to believe that lying immediately ahead was a period of relative peace. As for that impending change, it arrived when the king's absolute power was sharply curtailed, and parliamentary reform was inaugurated. Three years after the Lord Gordon Riots, in the wake of the loss of the American colonies, His Majesty in late 1783 arose to speak in Parliament about the latest jewel in the imperial crown when he said, "The situation will require the utmost exertion of your wisdom to contain and improve the valuable advantages derived from our Indian possessions."

Recovery and re-shuffling which would ensure the birth of a second empire in the east to replace the one lost in the west were simultaneously, and healthily, under way, and while British Intelligence organizations were to be active in India—throughout the East and Middle East for generations to come—another and very serious peril was looming much closer to home. Napoleon Bonaparte was becoming the menace to Britain no one since Philip of Spain had been, and which no one would be again until the rise of the Third Reich some one hundred and thirty years later.

And yet for all the pomp and power of the French Emperor, as far as Britain was concerned he had the personal misfortune of appearing a generation too late. Britain's economy had recovered, at least it could withstand the strains of another great war, and the same strategies which had failed in America did not necessarily have to fail on the Continent. British warships in the right numbers made possible an adequate defence against a Channel invasion, and compact, very professional British land forces under talented leaders made possible an engagement such as Waterloo when superior discipline, steadier ranks and an expert Intelligence factor granted victory to the best army in the right cause.

But several years before Waterloo, during the Russian campaign of 1812, the Czar's Intelligence organization broke Napoleon's *petit chiffre*, his 'little cipher', which enabled Russian generals to know in advance what the Emperor intended. This as much as any other single factor including that terrible winter of 1812, brought down disaster on the French when informed Russians, irregulars, Cossacks, and Kutusov's army, appeared along the route of withdrawal to take a consistent and deadly toll.

At the Battle of Leipzig the following year—16–19 October 1813 —the same thing happened again when the Emperor's splendid army, fresh from the victories of Lützen and Bautzen, 2 May and 20 May respectively, met the Alliance of Nations, Russia, Prussia and Austria, and was defeated.

Napoleon's code was simple. It consisted of one card with the alphabet printed upon it, and another card in the form of a sliding panel, which had the alphabet lettered twice upon it. The sliding panel was threaded through a pair of slits in the main card, until the key letter was aligned with the plaintext letter A of the stationery card. The other plaintext letters could then be encoded according to the letters below them.

Simplicity was the main advantage of the *petit chiffre*; almost anyone could encipher a message. And yet Napoleon's generals had difficulties. Several chose to completely ignore the cipher. Others never managed to use it correctly and still others half-coded their reports and messages.

Most fatal of all, this relatively uncomplicated cipher—called the St Cyr Code after the military academy Napoleon founded—was used incorrectly by a French general at Leipzig, which resulted in the Emperor's orders being disobeyed, and the battle was lost.

In 1815 during the hundred days British Intelligence read every message Napoleon sent, up to the fateful meeting at Waterloo which in June of 1815 completed the Emperor's downfall.

Uniquely, French black chambers—cryptographic bureaux—were among the most sophisticated and advanced in Europe. Also, the Emperor had a splendid Intelligence organization and was known to place great value on the espionage and counter-espionage talents of his spy-master Karl Shulmeister. Why then did he employ the simple St Cyr Code? Perhaps because he knew his commanders would scorn more complex ciphers. At least the *petit chiffre* was simple. Too simple it would seem.

Napoleon's predecessor Louis XIV, also an enemy of Great Britain, had a black chamber immediately adjoining his study at the palace of Versailles, and probably the greatest cryptanalyst of Europe was a Frenchman, Antoine Rossignol, who died in 1682 after revolutionizing the science of coding, so there was no apparent reason for Napoleon to have been neglectful in this area and yet he seems to have been.

Antoine Rossignol, incidentally, was able to decipher every coded message brought to him, and at least twice, once at the siege of Réalmont and again at the siege of La Rochelle, he deciphered messages handed to him on the spot, an occurrence which resulted in the fall of both cities.

Largely as a result of Rossignol's uncommon talent black chambers appeared throughout Europe in the seventeenth century. All nations likely to benefit from the secrecy of official correspondence sought among their own nationals people who could develop unsolvable ciphers.

In Vienna, capital of the extensive Holy Roman Empire, the *Geheime Kabinets-Kanzlei* (Secret Government Office) was one of the most accomplished black chambers in Europe. Before dawn the mail of all foreign embassies in the capital was delivered, opened, read, decoded, copied if necessary, re-sealed, returned to the mainstream of outgoing mail, and was subsequently delivered at breakfast time.

At the same time in the nineteenth century Britain's black chambers were also capable of baffling both friends and enemies. Experts at cryptology on the Continent, in the Middle East, the Indies and the Americas encountered British code variations which were largely the result of not just ingenious mathematics, but of the other essential—constant change.

British secret agents, it seemed, were everywhere. Africa, India, Europe, the Americas, north and south, and Asia. They established

Intelligence cadres among the employees of foreign governments, developed reliable sources of information in capitals, palaces, army commands, and at least once accomplished a spectacular coup by buying the co-operation of a foreign monarch, Catherine, the lusty Czarina of Russia. And in order to ensure that the tons of reports and messages got back to London with a minimum risk of revelation, they had to have adequate codes.

By the mid-1800s, after 300 years of empire-building, strong, rich, an epitome of successful democratic imperialism, Great Britain had developed so sensitive an Intelligence capability that nowhere on earth could an event occur which Whitehall did not know in advance was possible, and for which contingency plans did not exist.

Much of the information transmitted to and emanating from the Intelligence sector was conveyed by means of the Playfair Cipher, named after Baron Playfair who was a close associate of the code's developer, Sir Charles Wheatstone, a physicist and gifted mathematician, among whose scientific developments was an electric telegraph invented before Samuel Morse's version.

Wheatstone's cipher was explained at a state dinner by Baron Playfair at which were present Prince Albert, and a future Prime Minister, Lord Palmerston. The result was that the Wheatstone code was named after the man who popularized it, Baron Playfair, and it was subsequently adopted by the Intelligence service.

It was not as simple as the *petit chiffre*. In a Playfair cryptogram a square was formed by a key word, after which all the other letters of the alphabet were used to fill the square. Encipherment was arrived at through the use of paired letters. The plaintext letters, (in pairs) became the letter to their right or below them. Other pairs were replaced by a letter at the meeting of a column, or a row, which each pair was already in.

Put another way the Playfair Cipher required that a key word occupy the top line—and part of the second line if necessary—in any communication. There could be no utilization of a key word which required a duplication of letters, such as co*mm*odity or *everywh*ere. The balance of the square was then filled in with the alphabet. The letters I and J were treated as one letter, one symbol. To encode, the plaintext could then be scrambled to form adjoining digraphs, with an X dividing them in order to baffle decipherers who did not have a Playfair key.

There were variables to the Playfair Cipher which meant that in order to break the code someone had to first resolve, by locating a key, which variation was being employed. Time could be lost this way, and time was commonly of the essence in Intelligence work, particularly during military campaigns.

Playfair had a number of advantages in an era when sophisticated coding was approaching some kind of eighteenth-century zenith. The fact that in a Playfair plaintext digraphs obscured the frequency with which particular letters were used, put foreign cryptanalysts at a disadvantage. They could not employ a standard reference of every black chamber, the frequency tables.

Of course Playfair could be broken. There was never a code devised which Intelligence people could not break even though in some cases in order to secure the key they had to resort to bribery or some other means.

Nonetheless, Playfair was used by British Intelligence for a long time. What ultimately doomed nearly all the good eighteenth-century codes, and a great many which were developed in the twentieth century as well, was electronics, not, as historians have claimed, political reform.

Methods which were brought into being by electronic science enabled analysts to resolve code variables reaching into the hundreds of thousands, within hours or less. These same variables by human computation would require months and even years to resolve.

Sir Charles Wheatstone also developed a convenient little pocket-model encrypter for the spy who had everything. It somewhat resembled a pocket-watch, was encased in a hinged pocket-size case and consisted of two metal circles, a smaller one within a larger one. It had two sweeps, or 'hands', like the hour and second 'hands' of a watch.

The outer circle of the Wheatstone cryptograph contained the letters of the alphabet in proper sequence, with small numerals beneath most of the letters. The smaller or inner circle also contained letters of the alphabet but not in sequence.

By moving the main 'hand' to select letters a cipherer would also automatically move the other 'hand' because both 'hands' were integrated through gear propulsion. The result was that as the foremost 'hand' moved, the secondary 'hand' selected letters from the inner circle to be used as a code-letter or a word.

The long 'hand' in other words, viewed the plaintext, the other, lower 'hand', came up with a cipher-text equivalent.

As uncomplicated as this system was at first glance, because the letters could be altered to fit key words, the number of variables increased to create a considerable degree of difficulty for code-breakers, but as efficient as this system also was, it outlived its usefulness too.

In 1844 the British government let it be known that it no longer intercepted and read diplomatic correspondence. It was generally implied that the restricted power of monarchs, the enlightenment of ministers of state, the few serious hostilities in the world, had conspired together to make black chambers, and general espionage, unnecessary.

The Vienna black chamber was officially abolished in 1848. That same year France's *Cabinet Noir* was closed.

Over a hundred years later it was still being noted that in the 1840s Intelligence had become all but extinct in Europe, when in fact Britain's black chamber, all the British Intelligence operations had greatly expanded, while the French, Germans, Italians and Austrians during this same epoch of 'reform' had also considerably increased their secret services; not just in the size of operations but also in expertise.

Trade and industry did, as a matter of fact, dominate the latter half, as well as the middle, of the century, rather than as in the past, calamitous wars, at least for Britain. However for the governments of Melbourne, Peel, Russell and Palmerston, premiers under Queen Victoria, management of the last great empire of modern times required considerably more than pageantry, trade and enlightenment, it also required a considerable and on-going accumulation of secret information, something best supplied by an Intelligence community.

As trade increased, as the armed forces expanded, as commerce became strong and wealth accrued to Great Britain, so also did the need for a larger, more cosmopolitan Intelligence community. It was at that time and always had been, every nation's foremost vedette, and with the quiet appearance of more awesome weapons than before, no one could seriously expect others to believe, even a century later, that the secret services had diminished.

They had gone under a deeper cover. Never again would Intelligence budgets be either small nor readily discoverable. Nor would candour be an asset. From the middle of the nineteenth century to the early decades of the twentieth burgeoning militarism and the secret services grew apace, the one chillingly and increasingly visible, the other steadily less visible—not even acknowledged in fact—resulting in a condition of secrecy for the Intelligence community which only very recently has been subject to even partial exposure.

So successful has this wall of silence been that when great crises have been encountered, and formidable enemies met and conquered, not a word has appeared in popular histories about the contributions of the one service which has been responsible above other services, for someone's triumph, someone's loss.

8

The Maelstrom

Intelligence has always had as its basic concern the realities of political life, and assessments of Intelligence organizations have been based upon their efficiency and omniscience in comparison to the opposition.

In the area of political reality British Intelligence in Europe and the Americas during the middle and closing decades of the nineteenth century did not discern a single serious cloud upon the horizon. There were of course to be interludes of minor unpleasantness here and there—there always were—but nothing which seemed likely to assume critical proportions.

On that score, then, Britain's spy-masters could take heart. On the matter of comparison, they could feel equally assured. In places such as India and Africa where the second empire was flourishing, opposition Intelligence networks did not exist. Therefore comparison left the British Intelligence system looking very superior. It *was* one of the better networks. When it was compared to the French or German systems it still appeared better than mediocre, but when it was compared to the Irish underground with its meagre funding, inferior training but highly successful schemes, it looked less and less superior.

Nonetheless in the areas of the world where Britain held her main interests to be, Oceania, Asia, Africa and the Americas, the secret services seemed totally competent.

While political stability existed in the provinces, dependencies and colonies, there was still some dissent. That too was unavoidable. Very often dissenters were looked after by the 'Cavalry of St George', money from the government in the nature of gratuities—bribes.

At home those in government, as well as most others, were concerned with peace and stability. Not many felt compelled to ask how things were being accomplished, but it seemed quite clear that the British Intelligence sector was indeed capable, efficient, superior, and clearly doing its job.

For those outlying areas the system *was* superior. At the very least it was adequate. Except for two jolting exceptions; the Indian Mutiny of 1857 and the Boer War of 1899–1902.

It was the Boer War which created doubts at home, among them doubts as to the real efficiency of the Intelligence sector. Britain was at the apex of her power in 1899–1902. She maintained influence over roughly a third of the world. Her armies which in the past had been compact, small, and to an increasing degree mired in antiquated pageantry, were nonetheless magnificently disciplined and competently led—most of the time. And yet for all that, Great Britain required three years to conquer a handful of Dutch farmers.

Her Intelligence community had completely failed to assess correctly the temper and ability of the Boers, and out of this humiliation and minor tempest came the demands for reform which resulted in two distinct Intelligence organizations: M.I.1c, and M.I.5.

M.I.1c was responsible for espionage, and as it was later adapted to additional exigencies it became M.I.6. Military Intelligence 6, by which name it was to be known for a long while, so long in fact that it was still called M.I.6 when it had undergone another change of name, this time to Secret Intelligence Service, or S.I.S. implying severed connections with the military. It was also subsequently lumped with other Intelligence organizations under the 'secret service' nomenclature which was not only fairly appropriate, but which also facilitated discussion of the subject by people unfamiliar with nuances.

M.I.5, on the other hand (Military Intelligence 5) was created to handle counter-espionage, or Intelligence work as it existed at home, not abroad. But that of course created a problem. Since most alien secret agents, spies, Irish terrorists and the like, were not limited in their activities or their travels to the British Isles, agents of M.I.5, occasionally alone, but more often in connection with M.I.6, frequently left the country in the pursuit of their assignments.

M.I.5 was closely allied with Scotland Yard's Special Branch of the Police. In fact upon occasion the two agencies had interchangeable agents, and their relationship was usually of the kind which should exist between bureaux of government, something which did not always obtain between M.I.5 and M.I.6.

During the decades of the Empire M.I.5's limitation to counter-intelligence went beyond restriction to the British Isles. Dependencies, provinces and colonies were considered in this regard to be part of the nation.

Because M.I.6, the espionage arm, as opposed to M.I.5's counter-espionage concern, was also active 'out there', instances of overlapping occurred.

Ireland was an example. Because the Irish Republic did not exist until 1949, in earlier times Ireland was considered an M.I.5 province, but in fact M.I.6 had been discreetly at work there for some time. Irish independence received some impetus as early as 1923; enough to make the matter of independence something of a technicality, but problems there created a need for vigorous Intelligence activity, so not only did M.I.5 and M.I.6 appear, and remain, but so also did the police Special Branch, which at one time had no greater interest than Ireland.

An effort to avoid confusion, while defining not only the duties, spheres and responsibilities of Britain's Intelligence organizations but also the names, might be helpful, but not for long because Britain's secret service designations, as with those of all other countries, were subject to constant change. The Russians for example in about a half century went through Okhrana, Cheka, O.G.P.U., N.K.V.D., M.V.D. and most recently the K.G.B., and those were separate from such networks as the military G.R.U.

The point at issue is that while it may exasperate purists to categorize most of Britain's Intelligence operations simply as products of the 'secret service' it will certainly mitigate the confusion. And regardless of changed names, or even the number of times they are changed, in all the altered nomenclature there remains one constant; the purpose as well as duties of Intelligence personnel do not change.

Intelligence specialists, including those involved with cryptography, espionage, 'dirty tricks', counter-espionage, analysis and sabotage, any of the functions of their speciality, have traditionally performed according to age-old rules. Regardless of how a name-change may alleviate the blighted image of a particular organization, its personnel still operate as before. Intelligence work changes little, and not at all in its basic requirement: the accumulation of information.

Of course, and quite obviously, it changes in the methods used to get information. Sixty-five years ago the Kaiser's agents spied personally. Sixty-five years later German spies still performed as individuals, but most of their information was acquired and transmitted electronically. Mata Hari was out, fist-size electronic transmitters, bugs, spy-satellites, were in.

Most certainly the tools changed but in Britain, as elsewhere, the purpose of secret service did not change. Not even when its morality, as with the U.S. Central Intelligence Agency under the infamous Nixon administration, was made to reflect the offensiveness of a national leader. Or, as with Hitler's National Socialist Germany, when its purpose was perverted to serve and also to reflect the consummate evil of an even more invidious system, or, earlier in the same country's history, when the German Intelligence apparatus after the turn of the present century served the purpose of Wilhelm Hohenzollern so well; and also while the secret agents of Imperial Germany's antagonists repeatedly sent warnings home, which were just as repeatedly ignored.

Wilhelm's nationalist Germany, successor to Bismarck's newly created, proud and unified imperial German nation, was, in 1906–8, a model among successful monarchies. It was also called overbearing and self-centred. Perhaps with valid reason, except that Germany's neighbours were offended by arrogance and wary of spiked helmets. Still, that may not have been all that troubled the neighbours. Envy could have played a part.

The Germany Bismarck created—then bequeathed to Wilhelm when the chancellor fell in 1890—was rich, prosperous, powerfully and justifiably patriotic. It had reason to ridicule the inept French, the eternally disorganized and garrulous British, the clumsy Austro-Hungarian union, and the Italians.

After the turn of the century Germany was *the* power of Europe, which was unfortunate because it was also the most difficult—and powerfully armed—nation, and under Wilhelm was clearly going to become more, not less, difficult.

From 1896 and the episode of the Kruger telegram to the fateful day when Bismarck's splendid and wisely restricted German army left its proper niche under the Iron Chancellor, and under Wilhelm moved into the ruling councils, an event whose precedents throughout history have brought only tragedy, Germany's course was sadly predictable.

British Intelligence with eyes and ears inside the German chancellery reported the step-by-step advance of imperial nationalism under Wilhelm towards August 1914. But between 1908 and 1913 the Kaiser's intentions were increasingly obvious, without verification. Nor did he feel concern that France and Britain might discover his timetable. Like the old Austrian emperor when his son was assassinated, Wilhelm had cause to be pleased when at last his excuse to make war arrived.

The outbreak of the First World War of 1914–18 has been endlessly documented and detailed. Millions of dead, entire communities obliterated, ethnic groups annihilated, unprecedented devastation, economic ruin, all of it has been re-told in books by the hundreds, fixing blame, explaining strategies, even pinpointing sequences of no importance. Yet one insignificant event occurred in a French garden which not only altered the face of war, it changed the total human life style, after the war.

It occurred one month after the outbreak of war, in July 1914, behind the town hall of the village of Le Cateau in southern France.

Several men of the British Expeditionary Force's Army Intelligence Corps inside a parked lorry in the town-hall garden manipulated radio bands in an effort to accomplish what had never been done before; to intercept messages being transmitted by radio. In this instance the messages were being sent by nearby German army commanders. They were not coded messages. That would come later, when everyone used electronic interception as a matter of course.

Each message was translated into English and sent to B.E.F. headquarters, and for the first time an army's casualties soared, and its strategy and tactics were upset through the use of an invention which at that time was less than twenty years old; military electronics.

That lorry parked discreetly in the garden at Le Cateau was the initial phase of a discovery which was to revolutionize the Intelligence function. It gave unprecedented impetus to the secret agent's most difficult objective: getting his report back home safely and swiftly. It eliminated most of the risk run by couriers and intermediaries. Confidential information could be beamed over air waves with less hazard to the transmitter than ever before, and the degree of wastage among couriers, which was commonly higher than among actual spies, was eliminated altogether.

Of course the initial advantages did not last. German commanders quickly guessed how their plans were being upset, and after that the race was on. It is still on, and will continue into the predictable future. Nothing like the electronic revolution has ever occurred before.

There were other notable innovations to come out of the 'Great War'. Flying machines as weapons, improved photography, mass use of science, steel monsters which moved on treads instead of wheels, (tanks); ships which prowled the *underside* of the oceans. But nothing was to affect humanity in war and peace so much as the appearance and progress of electronics, and yet in 1914 it was to a great extent ignored. Among the Germans, who possessed several good Intelligence organizations, in the Foreign Offices as well as with the military, the general feeling—rightly—was that while spies were useful, what mattered were armies. Germany had the finest army in the world, the most skilled field marshals, why then should anyone feel obliged to need spies? No one, it seemed, recalled Napoleon's dictum that 'One spy in the right place is worth twenty thousand men on the battlefield'.

Erich von Ludendorff alone relied to a considerable extent upon Intelligence, and even he preferred moving against Germany's foes with a typically heavy hand. The German tradition rested upon a firm foundation of discipline and massed ranks.

Understandably, then, never during the course of the First World War were the Germans able to benefit as did the British from efficient and effective Intelligence. For a considerable period of time the Central Powers out-fought and out-thought the French and British, but in the fields of politics and diplomacy they blundered uninformedly from one gaffe to another. Their biggest oversight was to completely misread America, and that was fatal.

But misuse could be almost as fatal as non-use of Intelligence. When war came the British, regardless of ample early warning, were nowhere nearly as ready as they should have been. Yet the secret services moved before anyone else, so clearly not everyone was liable to confusion and procrastination. On the same day war was declared against Germany's Central Powers the British cable-ship *Telconia* steamed for the North Sea where on the fifth of August, 1914 she raised the German transatlantic cable, removed a considerable length of it, and steamed away.

The Germans did not control the North Sea, the British did.

Repairs were not attempted and as a result, for the duration of the war British Intelligence eavesdropped on German diplomats, and to a lesser extent upon the military and naval communications transmitted by conventional means.

Early in the war British Intelligence pioneered basic triangulation as a means for locating enemy headquarters on land and flotillas at sea. By 'fixing' the location of a radio transmitter and also by deducing from the variety of information being sent out or received, the size and importance of the station, it was possible for British Intelligence to inform assault groups where they might attack a German headquarters, supply depot, or warship, as at the Battle of Jutland.

But in this unprecedented war Intelligence could not be satisfied to make *a* difference; it had to make *the* difference. This was not a tidy, clever war, it was a vast, continent-wide charnel-house of a war. Even in the wake of the Second World War of 1939–45 the statistics of the 'Great War' were soberly impressive: nearly fifty million men in uniforms of some thirty nations, entire national populations recruited to sustain a war effort, and by 1918 when it was over, ten million men had been killed fighting and more than twice that number had been wounded, a high percentage disabled for life.

Nations were gone. The destruction had been so enormous and widespread no one before 1914 could have imagined it. The Americans, when they belatedly became involved, believed their boys would be home by Christmas. Kaiser Wilhelm told departing troops they would be home "before the leaves fall".

The war lasted four years and was from beginning to end an infantry struggle. Losses were unprecedented. In two battles, Verdun and the Somme, 1,800,000 men were killed and wounded on both sides. At Arras it cost the Allies 160,000 killed and wounded to advance 7,000 yards. Eight days later at Aisne the French were repulsed at a cost of 180,000 casualties.

At the Somme the British established a terrible record, unbroken to this time. Sixty thousand casualties in one day. During that offensive, which did not end until November 1916, and in which several miles of useless terrain were captured and held, the Allies, whose offensive it was, lost 794,000 men and the Germans lost 538,000.

That kind of war relied on one thing; walls of flesh and bone. It

Benedict Arnold persuades Major André to conceal papers in his boot

Baron Playfair after whom the
'Playfair' cypher was named

Sir Charles Wheatstone, the scientist who invented the 'Playfair' cypher

Sir William Reginald Hall (*standing second from right*) director of Naval Intelligence in the First World War, entertaining one of his old enemies Count Felix von Luckner, in 1935

was a land conflict of big battalions, great armies, and over-powering offensives. It relied for results on weapons which downed masses of men; the machine-gun, point-blank artillery—and gas.

But no nation could stand those losses for long. National populations were unable to withstand the drain. In 1914 the British committed their regular army to the Western front. In early 1915 it had ceased to exist. Britain then had to raise an army by conscription of a million men, from a population of approximately forty-five million people and although 65 per cent of Britain's armed forces came from the British Isles, only 35 per cent coming from the colonies, provinces and dependencies, 80 per cent of the casualties came from the British Isles, losses of roughly two and a half million from a population of forty-five million.

The entire conflict was on a comparable scale. When the Russians invaded eastern Prussia in the summer of 1914 with two armies totalling about half a million men, the Germans struck them under Paul von Hindenburg at Tannenberg, and Russian casualties were 300,000 before the defeat turned into a rout.

Conscription helped but not for long, for the British this conflict was to be the turning point in history. Never before had the nation been required to mobilize, and to squander, all its resources; money, men, seagoing strength and industrial capacity. From this wholesale outpouring she would never recover. What all this amounted to was simply that the male population of Europe's committed countries would never be adequate for the drain.

The masses of Russia which under different circumstances—more competent leaders, more modern equipment, professional training and adequate supplies—might have been able to tip the scales, simply went down to defeat, demoralized and confused every time they might have withstood defeat. For the Allies this was the ultimate discouragement.

The Italians were even less dependable. Anyone accepting them as allies would have been served better by coaxing Italy's leaders to join the opposition.

That left the French to contain the Germans, which they did with British help, in 1914, and when France all but collapsed in 1915, the British were left holding back Kaiser Wilhelm's hordes alone, but it was clear by mid-1915 the war was not going to be won by stalemate or containment, therefore a fresh source of wealth, weapons and above all else, manpower, had to be found.

One such source existed. The United States of America. It was rich, huge, second only to Russia in size among the warring nations, had a large pool of war-age manpower, was capable of vast industrial production, and culturally as well as linguistically was bound to Great Britain.

It also happened to be peace-loving, with a very small army and navy, and had since the beginning of the war in Europe, been awed by the scale of the campaigns, and the losses. There were Americans, some in high office, who opposed any involvement in Europe's problems.

For Britain in particular but also for the Central Powers, the question became one of devising a way to jolt the Americans out of their neutrality.

Britain needed America as an ally. Germany was never that hopeful, but if the Americans could be kept neutral the Germans were confident how their war would end.

For the Germans, then, the problem was to devise a diversion, for the British the problem was to devise a *causus belli*. Both turned to their Intelligence departments for an answer, and finally the difference between the German Intelligence community and the much stronger, more seasoned British apparatus was to not only settle the matter of superiority, it was also to demonstrate clearly that while armies fought wars, under some circumstances it was the Intelligence operation which enabled one army to triumph over others.

9

The Cliff-Hangers

By 1917 the paralysing losses had for the Germans emphasized the fact that barring some daring stroke of genius, some sudden, overwhelming assault which would put them in Paris amid a fallen France and a crumbling Britain where they could quickly impose terms of peace, they were not likely to win the war. Unlike the enemy, whose importunities might bring America to the battlefields with fresh armies, Germany had only her own population to conscript, and after the years of stunning attrition the bottom of that barrel was clearly in sight.

The Kaiser's strategy then, was compelled to assume a new, and clearly desperate, relevance. France would fall if Britain could be crippled, but despite horrendous losses the British showed no indication of crumbling. Wilhelm's Foreign Office went to work. It had contingency plans by the score, exactly as it also had dozens of ciphers. Cryptography, of late, had made great strides, as it had had to do after the Germans discovered how expert their enemies had become in this area.

At about the same time, the Americans were involved in a bandit-hunt in Mexico, with permission of Mexican President Carranza, for a sometime-revolutionary, more often brigand, named Francisco Villa; called 'Pancho' by an admiring Mexican following.

Fifteen thousand American soldiers under General John J. Pershing were involved. Despite official Mexican sanction this was not a popular event in Mexico where, in the spring of 1914 United States Marines had fought their way into, and occupied, the port city of Vera Cruz to prevent a German ship from unloading munitions. War nearly erupted over that escapade and most Mexicans were still antipathetic towards the United States when the hunt for Villa was undertaken.

United States President Wilson stopped the manhunt and recalled Pershing's expeditionary force late in 1916, which eased the immediate tension but did not to any noticeable degree alleviate anti-Americanism in Mexico.

There did not appear to be even a slight connection between this posse-like American undertaking and the prodigious struggle in Europe, but there was. At least one was created by the German Foreign Office whose plan to divert the Americans through pre-occupation in their own hemisphere created a crisis with unexpected side effects.

By 1917 there was considerable ill will in the United States towards Germany. It was a reciprocal situation, but at least in America, where tales of atrocities, mostly untrue, were common-place, the advent of Germany's undersea campaign confirmed for many Americans the diabolism of Wilhelm's government.

That submarine fleet was in 1917 the largest in the world with over a hundred boats of which eighty operated in the waters off the British Isles. In April 1917, alone, German U-boats sent to the bottom 875,000 tons of Allied shipping—largely British—with a considerable loss of life. By the end of the year the total would reach eight million tons.

American reaction to submarines was unfavourable, even before they ran up such terrible tolls. But with a pacifist President in the White House, American animosity towards the Central Powers lacked both effective leadership and strong direction.

Meanwhile in Berlin, battlefield events bordering upon desperation brought Wilhelm's Foreign Office into the crisis with a two-fold plan. Foremost was agreement with the military—strongly influenced at this time by von Ludendorff, Hindenburg's chief of staff—that Britain must be brought to her knees at home since she was clearly not going to be defeated in battle. It was proposed to accomplish this by unrestricted submarine warfare in the waters around the British Isles, whose purpose would be to create a threat of starvation. To isolate Britain, the supply ships of her friends, or from neutral ports, would be sunk before they could reach British docks. This would also, so the reasoning went, result in demoralization among British troops in France.

That was the first phase of the Foreign Office strategy. It was fiercely opposed by some Germans including Chancellor Bethmann-Holweg and his Foreign Minister Gottlieb von Jagow. Their conviction was that unrestricted submarine warfare against neutral vessels carrying supplies to Britain, many of which were American, would bring America into the war.

Those favouring the plan pointed out that even without the known pacifism of Woodrow Wilson, the United States Army and Navy were insignificant. Also, if the United States suddenly became engulfed in the war, its preparations would take up to a year, by which time Britain could be starved to submission and France, which was by 1917 nearly completely exhausted, could be beaten on the battlefields.

But there was no unanimity of opinion even among Germany's military leaders. Paul von Hindenburg opposed "ruthless war". Generals Mackensen and von Ludendorff approved. Both were American-phobes. Mackensen in particular was an *Amerikaner-fresser* (American-hater).

Also in opposition was Count Johann Heinrich von Bernstorff the German Ambassador to the United States. He warned that it would almost certainly result in a declaration of war by the American government. He also seems to have been in opposition on moral grounds.

It was also suggested that Germany's U-boats would frighten the Americans. That was proved incorrect in October 1916 when the U-53 sank six vessels off Nantucket as a clear warning, and the American reaction was swift and fierce.

No one, it seemed, doubted Germany's ability to blockade the British Isles, and while this phase of the two-pronged plan was under anxious discussion, particularly in London, the second phase was plotted, and here the Americans were to make a great mistake. They assumed that Alfred Zimmerman who had replaced von Jagow as Foreign Minister in November 1916, would continue von Jagow's policy of opposition to *rücksichtlose Krieg*, because earlier, as von Jagow's immediate subordinate—under chief secretary for Foreign Affairs—he had echoed von Jagow's sentiments.

But it was Alfred Zimmerman who demonstrated a degree of prescience when he said, "The American neutrality toward Germany is one of the head; toward the Allies it is one of the heart. What America does for the Allies she does voluntarily and gladly; what she does for Germany she does because she must."

But, as a matter of fact, Zimmerman did initially side with Bethmann-Holweg and von Jagow in opposition to unrestricted warfare. Only when he succeeded von Jagow did he become an advocate of the general plan, which incidentally was supported by Germany's field-marshals, and Kaiser Wilhelm.

Very shortly the Americans were to discover just how badly they had misjudged this big, broad, direct, forceful and magnetic man with the duelling scars. In was Alfred Zimmerman who now implemented the second phase of the general plan, which was to go into effect at about the same time as the blockade of Britain.

The Japanese, who had overrun German possessions on China's mainland as well as in the Pacific in 1914, when there was little danger of retaliation or resistance, were approached with an offer of alliance and a free hand in Asia and Siberia, as well as something of the same kind down the west coast of the United States, in exchange for a declaration of war against the Americans.

Japan procrastinated, but Japanese warships steamed along the United States coast as far south as Mexico, and in Berlin this action was construed as a propitious harbinger.

Then Zimmerman expounded his personal views of another source of potential comfort to the Kaiser's government. He repeated what he had often said, that there were at least "five hundred thousand trained Germans ready to bear arms in the United States against the American government".

In 1916 when he made this pronouncement within the hearing of the United States Ambassador, James W. Gerard, he received this reply: "There may be, but there are five hundred thousand lamp-posts to string them up to if they ever try it."

Whether Zimmerman believed a 'fifth column' existed or not, he knew where the American soft under-belly was. In less than a month after he became Foreign Minister, the civil government which he strongly influenced was ready to collaborate with the military leadership to minimize any danger likely to face Germany from the Western Hemisphere. The American reaction to the proposal for unrestricted warfare, brought to United States attention by British Intelligence which had verbatim orders to U-boat commanders to pass along, was exactly what Zimmerman had predicted, a lot of loud, angry talk.

On 17 January 1917 Alfred Zimmerman, employing Code 0075 sent a message to the German Ambassador in Mexico City outlining the plan for unrestricted submarine warfare, and also the second phase of the German general plan, a proposal that Mexico become Germany's ally against the United States. In exchange for this she would receive financial credits, plus the return of her former territories of Texas, New Mexico and Arizona, taken from her in 1848 at the conclusion of the Mexican-American War.

From beginning to end the sending of this message was folly. The reasons were many and obvious. After the British cut Germany's transatlantic cable in 1914, the Germans requested permission of the pro-German Swedes to use the Stockholm-London-Washington cable and when the British protested, Sweden's leaders yielded, but instead they gave the Germans access to their Stockholm-Buenos Aires link. From Argentina the Germans could transmit over their own cable to Mexico City and Washington. This was the 7,000 mile so-called 'Swedish Roundabout'.

But Germany also had access to a second route, the United States diplomatic cable. German guile convinced President Wilson that the Kaiser's genuine search for peace would be best promoted if there were an avenue of communication open between Washington and Berlin, as there was between Washington and London.

The Americans even agreed to allow German messages to be transmitted in German codes. Washington's *naïveté* could have been pardoned. They were still employing a code devised by Thomas Jefferson over a hundred years earlier. But Germany's Foreign Office should have known better. Both the United States cable and the 'Swedish Roundabout' were vulnerable. Both touched London, one directly, one indirectly. London, it was common knowledge, was the base of the world's most accomplished cryptanalysts.

The British had been eavesdropping on Washington for several years, monitoring both the diplomatic cable and the telegraph system. Also, since their Admiralty Intelligence section, Room 40, had intercepted, decoded, and read instructions to the U-boat commanders over a considerable length of time, as well as diplomatic messages emanating from Berlin and destined for all parts of the world, its cryptanalysts could almost tell at a glance which code or cipher was at hand after an interception.

Zimmerman compounded his blunder by using both the diplomatic cable and the commercial telegraph system. He must have been confident that Code 0075 was inviolate. There was some justification for this as 0075 was complex and possessed 10,000 variables. But it had also been in use a long time.

In command of Room 40 at Whitehall was Captain William Reginald Hall, an outstanding Royal Navy officer whose impaired health had brought his sea-duty to an end when he was re-assigned to the Admiralty's Intelligence Bureau.

Under Captain Hall was a bizarre selection of people. One cryptographer was an ordained churchman, another had an interest in fashion designing and another was a music critic.

The church historian, William Montgomery, and Nigel de Grey, a talented mathematician and publisher, both of the Political Section, were handed Zimmerman's intercepted message on the morning of 17 January 1917. Both had been working on German codes 0075 and 13040 for some time. They were able to recognize an interception in 0075 on sight. They had in fact been decoding 0075 intercepts on the cable the Swedes had assured the British they would not allow the Germans to use. It was proper to protest, but it was also practical to arrange a tap and listen in.

Code 0075, like all codes, was a method of exchanging one complete word for another, or scrambling letters and numbers in place of words. The key was that both sender and receiver had to possess copies of the same code book. There were methods of simplification by which coding and decoding could be expedited, but in general Code 0075 was not a simple code. For example a word might be designated by the numbers 24767. Another word, as an addendum, could be 24768. The cryptanalysts had to break down the first five numbers. If 24767 meant 'airplane', for example 24768 could mean airplane*s*. Once the proper designation of a set of numbers was decoded, it allowed the decoders to work from a base. But the Germans, who were also very adept, changed their codes often. Near the end of the war they were changing them daily, scrambling numbers, letters, and switching code books, so the dilemma became an endless one.

Still, when Zimmerman's message was lifted from the Swedish cable it was recognized as an 0075 transmission, and shortly afterward that same morning a second message was lifted from the United States cable. These became messages 157 and 158. Both appeared to be identical and both were addressed to Count von Bernstorff, the German Ambassador in Washington.

William Montgomery and Nigel de Grey were not working entirely in the dark on their assignment. They had already verified, for example, that in Code 0075 the grouping 4280 designated the German Foreign Office. (In Code 13040 it was 97556.) They also knew that 4852 referred to Foreign Minister Alfred Zimmerman.

Clearly, messages 157 and 158 were in substance the same. Just as clearly they were top-level, secret communications. The figures 5841 meant top secret but that in itself was no proof as all coded or ciphered messages had some such designation.

Nor was the labour of Room 40 made easier by the fact that the word 'stop', used in place of a period in most cable and wireless communications was seldom the same because the Germans knew as well as the Britons that any set of numbers used repeatedly, could be broken down and assigned other letters or words, their components then used by comparison to break down other words or letters.

There were various clusters used for 'stop' but de Grey and Montgomery had progressed this far in their earliest studies. They knew the 'stop' alternatives. They also knew several key alphabetical and numerical arrangements. And because Montgomery was an accomplished linguist in German, the solution to problems created by men who thought in that language was additionally facilitated.

In a subsequent message sent by Count Bernstorff to Ambassador Eckhardt in Mexico City in Code 13040 relaying Zimmerman's message, Nigel de Grey was able to recognize the grouping 13042 as a 13040 variant. Room 40 had a 13040 code book—from the bottom of the ocean—and using it, by 10.30 a.m. 17 January 1917, only a few hours after de Grey and Montgomery had been assigned the task, they had a partial decoding completed. They handed it to Captain Hall. It read as follows:

> Most secret for Your Excellency's personal information and to be handed to the Imperial Minister in —— with Telegram No 1 —— by a safe route.
> We propose to begin on the 1st February unrestricted submarine warfare. In so doing we shall endeavour to keep America neutral. —— If we should not (be able to do so) we propose to —— an alliance upon the following basis:
> (Joint?) conduct of the war.
> (Joint?) conclusion of the peace.
> ————
> Your Excellency shall for the present inform the President of —— (we expect war?) with the USA ——. —— and at the same time to negotiate between us and Japan —— that —— or submarines —— will compel England to peace in a few months. Acknowledge receipt. Zimmerman.

The nation which de Grey and Montgomery had difficulty decoding was Mexico. The proper name eventually fell into place, and with that cleared up Admiral Hall had in his hand the key which was almost certain to unlock the door of America's 'arsenal of democracy'.

It helped when Bernstorff's reply in Code 13040 was intercepted. He was not in sympathy with his government's new policy, but he obeyed orders and saw to it that those to be informed were accordingly contacted.

Five days later when President Wilson went before the Congress with his "peace without victory" address, the personnel at Room 40 in London had their word-perfect translation of the Zimmerman message completed. On 1 February, Germany began unrestricted submarine warfare. The difficulty for Room 40 was twofold. First, the United States had to be convinced of the authenticity of the Zimmerman message—no easy accomplishment as other Allied efforts at involving the United States had made America's leaders suspicious of *all* efforts. Secondly, if Room 40's revelation came to Washington in the nature of an Intelligence report, within days of the transmission of Berlin's top secret instructions, the Germans would realize British Intelligence had broken their codes, which would result in swift abandonment and creation of fresh codes.

Respecting the first problem—American belief—the Germans would take care of that themselves on 1 February when they inaugurated unrestricted submarine warfare.

As for protecting the existence and expertise of Room 40, Intelligence Section took care of that. A British spy in Washington procured a copy of the Zimmerman telegram from the office of Count Bernstorff. Another secret agent, in Mexico City, secured a second copy from the Western Union commercial telegraph office. Both of these were in Code 13040. This information was given to the Americans, who did not know Room 40 existed.

Very shortly afterwards unrestricted submarine warfare began. Also very shortly afterwards British Intelligence assisted the American Intelligence in creating a genuine copy of the Zimmerman note, without which it was feared the American leadership would believe the entire affair was another British ruse.

German code books along with the original interceptions were loaned to Edward Bell, United States Intelligence attaché at the Grosvenor Square offices of the American Embassy. Bell's translation, made by an American in an American embassy, was convincing. More convincing, by mid-February, was the cold-blooded, ruthless stalking of all ships other than those of the Central Powers by killer packs of German submarines.

During March the Americans carefully verified what had come to them from British Intelligence. That same month the American President Woodrow Wilson went through an ordeal of soul-searching. He was a dogged pacifist to the last. Finally, in March the decoded, translated copies of Zimmerman's message were published in United States newspapers with a predictable result. As Count Bernstorff had been trying to convince his government, the Americans exploded in fierce and articulate indignation.

On 2 April 1917, with bands of dissenting pacifists roaming the American capital, President Wilson went before the Congress at 8 o'clock in the evening. He told a packed, hushed house:

> The present German submarine warfare against commerce is a warfare against mankind. American ships have been sunk, American lives taken, which it has stirred us very deeply to learn of, but the ships and people of other neutral and friendly nations have been sunk and over-whelmed in the water in the same way. There has been no discrimin-ation. The challenge is to all mankind. Each nation must decide for itself how it will meet it. . . .
> There is one choice we cannot make, we are incapable of making, we will not choose the path of submission and suffer the most sacred rights of our nation and our people to be violated and ignored. The wrongs against which we now array ourselves are not common wrongs; they cut to the very root of human life. . . . I advise that the Congress declare the recent course of the Imperial German Government to be in part nothing less than war against the people of the United States; that it frankly accept the status of belligerent . . . . It is a fearful thing to lead this great, powerful people into war—the most terrible and disastrous of all wars, civilisation itself seems to be in the balance. . . .

The chamber of Congress arose as one person. The cheering was deafening. According to a spectator: "The whole assembly was on its feet. From its throat an ardent and deep cry" erupted.

Elsewhere throughout the nation Wilson's declaration was over-whelmingly approved, not always with cheering, but often with full agreement that the nation could no longer remain neutral, a condi-tion which, so historians have said ever since, would have come about eventually in any case, but which most certainly *did* come about in April 1917 as a result of the blunder of Foreign Minister Zimmerman in Berlin, and the ability of Admiralty Room 40 at Whitehall.

On 6 April 1917 the United States declared war on Germany. Not until the following 7 December did she declare war on Austria-

Hungary. The delay was the result of British Intelligence revealing to the Americans that the Austro-Hungarian Emperor Charles and his Foreign Minister Czernin were secretly in touch with London and Paris seeking to reach a separate peace agreement.

The affair came to nothing, primarily because of intransigence on both sides, and the United States ultimately declared war on Austria-Hungary as one of the Central Powers.

10

The Un-Healing

There were two clear results of America's entry into the war. One was a re-alignment of international power, never again within the view of modern man would a European concert of nations dominate the world.

The other result was that isolation became a casualty too. Europe had committed a form of suicide; political and to some extent social. Europeans might for a short while believe, after the departure of the last American and Russian soldier, that their lives would begin anew within the old contexts, but they would not. The shadow of one or the other, Russia or America, would linger for generations.

And the Americans *had* made the difference. They left behind rows upon rows of little white crosses—fifty thousand casualties, a fraction of British losses and France's million and a half *poilus*, but they *had* arrived, they *would* fight, and their presence doomed Imperial Germany.

About the time von Ludendorff surprised everyone—including himself—with the success of his 9 April offensive which drove ten miles before being halted by Foch's French and Haig's British in the Hazebrouck-Ypres area, a dozen United States divisions had arrived in France. At that time the Allies had almost no reserves and the Germans although fighting with two hundred and ten divisions did not possess a single division which was at full strength.

Before Ludendorff's offensive was contained the British had been decimated; three hundred thousand casualties. One hundred and forty thousand replacements were hurried over from England.

The Americans were finally ready to go into the line. They had fresh troops, excellent equipment, and an assurance of many more divisions to come. For the Germans the sands were running out. But they tried again, in the Reims-Soissons sector, fifteen German divisions against seven Allied divisions, and as before although the tactical success was outstanding the strategic victory eluded them.

The first American shell fell on the German lines 23 October 1917. At that stage Americans appeared in the trenches, but it was not before 21 January 1918 that a major segment of the front—an eight-mile stretch of it north-west of Nancy—was completely manned by Americans replacing the French.

Failure dogged the Germans, unrelenting though they were. On 8 August General von Ludendorff said this was "the black day of the German army. . . . It put the decline of our fighting power beyond all doubt. . . . The war must be ended."

But it did not end. Bulgaria collapsed 29 September 1918 and Ludendorff said this "sealed the fate of the Quadruple Alliance", but Germany fought on.

Turkey capitulated 30 October and that same day the Austrians asked for terms, which were given, and signed into effect 4 November. Still Germany fought.

Revolution broke out inside Germany in the first week of November, at the same time German Intelligence reported that the Allies were now preparing to attack from the rear, through defeated Austria. Simultaneously there was a steady advance from the west.

Ludendorff said he wanted to save what remained of the army, and at the Foreign Office in Berlin there was talk of deposing the Kaiser and asking for immediate peace.

By October there were 2,085,000 American troops in France; forty-two divisions, of which thirty-two were ready for battle. Germany had roughly one-third of that number of divisions, but because German divisions had not been at full strength in over a year, the disparity was even greater.

Germany requested terms. They were offered. At 5 a.m. 11 November 1918 an armistice was signed in a railway carriage in the Compiegne Forest. At 11 o'clock that morning the First World War ended. The Allies had triumphed. President Wilson who had been trying for several years to achieve a "peace without victory" simply in order to stop the slaughter, may have provided the correct term respecting the peace; no one had 'won' it; it *was* a 'peace without victory' but not for a decade and more would that be apparent. What the end of the war *did* accomplish, apart from the reduction of all major combatants to the role of paupers, was to prove quite convincingly that great men, in war or in peace, were always fallible, frequently treacherous, and never to be trusted.

No war, it was said, to gain whatever ends, was worth what this one had cost, and along with widespread political disillusionment went social upheaval. Bolsheviks not only overthrew the Russian Czar, they murdered him. They tried to do the same with God but over the ensuing years He put to use the craftiness learned over the preceding millennia; they simply could not pin Him down.

They also embarked upon a fresh epoch of conquest. There was always someone—there had always been someone—to move into the kind of vacuum left by the war. The new Russians employed all means short of conflict, at first, to spread their ideology, until they were strong—and unified enough—they they too would resort to arms.

They entered the era of exhaustion and confusion as providential opportunistic totalitarianists who professed to be the absolute opposite, and the radicals from *their* system were nihilists, seekers after anarchy, terrorists asking only an opportunity to betray *any* order. It helped their cause that millions of people who still preferred living within the framework of some kind of social order, would nonetheless have nothing to do with politics, politicians or ideologies, systems of any kind. They wanted to turn their backs on any kind of benumbing sadism which could cost ten million human lives.

This revulsion also existed in high places. The Allied nations could not be rid of war's weighty panoply quickly enough. Armies faded, navies went into dry-dock, the brilliant men of Room 40 returned to civilian life, even the Admiralty's Intelligence Division as a whole, seemed superfluous in an era when no one could see any kind of armed resurgence immediately ahead. Certainly Germany, whose cities lay in ashes, whose social, economic and political structures were hopelessly ruined, could not rise again. And Russia in her Bolshevik paroxysm was helpless, and as for the Bolshevik export, mindless proletarianism, it need never be taken seriously.

Intelligence work was considered less likely than almost anything to be of value, and as they always had, the secret services reflected social and political mores. In a world of shattered values and emergent but obscure fresh ideologies, the secret services were viewed as being as useless as a standing army on a continent which had only exhausted nations, and no enemies at all.

The existence of this providential interregnum makes possible exploration among the direct and indirect aspects of Intelligence during the closing phase of the war, and some of the unique results of the professionalism gained during and immediately afterwards.

For example the former British consul Roger Casement, an Irish patriot, worked diligently to secure German support for an Irish rebellion while England was totally committed on the Continent. Room 40 intercepted messages to Casement from the German Foreign Office. These in turn led to cables to the Foreign Office from Casement, using the United States cable.

Room 40 cryptanalysts defined the code and when it seemed imminent that Casement would be put ashore in Ireland from a German submarine, it was determined that if the word 'Hay' were in a message, Casement would *not* be on board, but if the word 'Oats' appeared, Casement *would* be aboard.

With that information at hand Room 40 waited, and when an interception was made on 12 April 1916 which included the word 'Oats' a close watch was begun, and ten days later after Roger Casement was put ashore in Ireland, he was arrested.

It was very good Intelligence, but with a sad ending. Roger Casement was convicted of high treason within three months, and hanged.

Room 40 was also instrumental, through coded interceptions, in bringing a German spy named Margarete Zell to her death before a French firing-squad. She was commonly known as Mata Hari.

Additionally, when the Americans became involved in establishing an Intelligence system, Admiralty and other British secret services lent professional assistance.

United States Intelligence made excellent progress under its first strong advocate, a young Indianan named Herbert Osborne Yardley. When the United States entered the war, Yardley succeeded in convincing the War Department to authorize the establishment of a bureau of cryptanalysis and code-breaking—a black chamber. This was designated the Military Intelligence Division, and in the English tradition was called 'M.I.8', or plain MI8.

With America at war MI8 grew considerably. It handled coded messages from the United States west coast, southward to Mexico where United States spies were especially watchful after the episode of the Zimmerman note, and throughout Central and South America. Its panel of analysts, again like the British, consisted of some very unlikely personnel including one man who was an authority on Chaucer, a philologist named John Manly. He and an assistant, Edith Rickert, broke the code of a German taken into custody in Mexico in connection with sabotage, who had in his possession when captured a rather lengthy message. The German's name was Lothar Witzke.

It required three days to decode the Witzke note, which was a twelve-step transposition signed by the German Ambassador to Mexico, Heinrich von Eckhardt.

Witzke's protestation of innocence ended when Dr Manly handed the decoded message to his superiors. It read: "The bearer of this message is a subject of the Empire [German] who travels as a Russian under the name of Pablo Waberski. He is a German secret agent. Please furnish him on request protection and assistance; also advance him on demand up to 1000 pesos of Mexican gold and send his code telegram to this embassy."

Witzke was convicted of espionage and sentenced to death. He languished in United States prisons until five years after the war, then was released and sent home.

Captain Yardley's concern was less with German codes and ciphers than it was with intercepted Japanese communications. His black chamber was the principal cause for joint United States-British intransigence at the post-war world conference on naval tonnage. When Japan's representatives stood firm on a 10:7 ratio, Britain and the United States stood firm at 10:6. Yardley's organization had intercepted and decoded instructions to Japan's emissaries to demand 10:7 but to settle for 10:6.

The efficiency of America's black chamber resulted in a degree of in-government notoriety, something most secret services have preferred to avoid. Yardley's panel of experts broke the codes of Russia, Germany, Japan, Great Britain, France, China, and a number of Latin American countries, but as memory of the Great War faded with the advent of the Great Depression, and MI8 became less and less a secret, an ideal excuse was found for its abolition when the United States government embarked upon a programme of economization. Captain Yardley's black chamber was closed down in 1929.

However, consistent with common practice, MI8's demise masked the work of the United States Army's Signal Corp Intelligence Service, whose function was the same as had been Yardley's black chamber: to prepare codes and ciphers for the

United States and to intercept and break foreign codes in war and peace.

The Signal Intelligence Service was under a civilian, its ostensible founder and organizer, Russian-born William Frederick Friedman. An associate in the profession of code-breaking, Elizabeth Smith, became Mrs Friedman in 1917. In fact this couple was called upon several times even before Yardley's black chamber was organized, to decode United States government interceptions.

William Friedman coined the word 'cryptanalyst'. He was one of America's outstanding professionals, a man of many talents. One of his discoveries, in 1917, led to the exposure of a bizarre plot to embarrass the British who at that time were fully committed on the Continent.

German instructions and funds forwarded by diplomatic code to the leader of a band of East Indians in the United States revealed that the Indians planned to purchase weapons in the United States, and, back in India, foment a popular uprising.

William Friedman knew the German diplomatic code. He turned his report over to the government, the Indians were apprehended and put on trial in Chicago and San Francisco.

The highlight of the San Francisco trial occurred when one of the conspirators, in the act of turning State's evidence in exchange for a promise of clemency, was suddenly fired upon by another of the Indian defendants who had somehow managed to bring a handgun into the courtroom. The testifying conspirator was killed. The man who shot him was then shot and killed by a fast-drawing United States marshal in the back of the courtroom, who had to fire over the heads of the seated spectators.

Sometime after this affair the British, who were experimenting with one of the Intelligence operations' most unique and promising innovations, an enciphering teleprinter, sent a short message to William Friedman, in cipher. The same day he received the British challenge, Friedman cabled back the plaintext, which read: "This cipher is absolutely indecipherable."

So much for that particular enciphering machine.

But in the 1930s, coding and enciphering machines, the early ones of which resembled typewriters, were being developed and tested by every major Intelligence organization. Japan, on the march in China and elsewhere, developed a machine called the '97-shiki-O-bon In-ji-ki' or 'Alphabetical Typewriter 2597'.

Meanwhile, for Britain, whose post-war years had been full of such pressing problems as demobilization, unemployment and financial woes of considerable proportions, all of it in a world of seething discord and disunion, there were the perennial 'Irish troubles'.

There were to arise from this two noticeable features. One, perhaps the foremost factor, was that the Irish disturbance was a conflict of the secret services, British and Irish. The second feature was that as early as 1918 Britain, meaning essentially England, was to experience the first series of terrorist campaigns of the present century.

For the dissenting Irish, Germany's defeat in 1917 meant simply a switch of direction in the search for an ally. What the German Foreign Office had been unable to deliver, the rebelling Irish now were to seek from the United States with greater hope of achievement, not entirely because America was rich and presumably sympathetic, but also because it had a large Irish-American population.

For the English, who had no doubts of the outcome if they could manoeuvre the Irish Republican Army into a conventional fight, the problem very quickly evolved into a sniping match among hit-and-run antagonists; terrorist-style combat. This, then, required an approach through the Intelligence networks, and that became a lengthy, demoralizing matter, basically because, one could assume, as with the American Loyalists during the Rebellion, the opposition was powerfully motivated by ideology; there were almost no turncoats. Betrayal was encouraged when London put an exorbitant price on the head of Michael Collins—£10,000 dead or alive—but even that temptation did not entice a traitor, so the embattled English had to rely more than ever on the variety of traditional secret service which was popular in earlier times: infiltration by individual espionage agents. But the Irish had an Intelligence network of their own. It consisted largely of ideological sympathizers, and for that reason was quite extensive. It even managed to operate in London—enemy territory.

For Whitehall the procedure followed conventional rules, up to a point. The secret agents employed, came from Scotland Yard's Special Branch, from the Dublin Metropolitan Police, and also from M.I.6 and M.I.5 (the Secret Intelligence Service).

Throughout the 1920s the see-sawing went on without respite, and the better-funded, larger government forces were more often than not checkmated by what may have been no more than thirty or forty I.R.A. activists among a population of native sympathizers without whose aid and comfort the struggle could never have continued. Although English penetration did occasionally succeed, Commandant Collins's own secret infiltration squads demonstrated their ability by, in turn, placing spies within the Dublin Metropolitan Police organization, especially G. Division which was the detection unit, meaning that I.R.A. Intelligence knew almost at once when secret agents arrived from London, or when S.I.S. officers were to appear.

Another Irish cadre consisted of assassins. It occasionally happened that when spies inside the D.M.P. reported on the identity of S.I.S. people the assassins would be dispatched. On 21 November 1920 this happened with resounding effect. A number of S.I.S. officers were assassinated, some of them in their beds in the very early morning, before the eyes of their families.

Incredibly, that same afternoon an Irish crowd at a sporting event was suddenly machine-gunned in retaliation and this act of mindless vengeance did more to crystallize not just Irish but world-wide hostility, than those murders earlier in the day.

The results were far-reaching; Britain's Parliament in December passed the Government of Ireland Act, a prelude to independence, but in more distant parts of the Empire other dissidents were encouraged by Irish tactics, and Irish successes. Nor were the expansion-minded Japanese blind to the kind of accomplishments against Britain's government that Ireland's terror campaign had produced. They were to emulate I.R.A. infiltration, fifth-column techniques in the years ahead, but that was still more than a decade into the future. In the 1920s Great Britain's concerns lay elsewhere than in Asia, although she had possessions there.

For one thing the deferred costs of a war which had been unstintingly waged for more than four years were calling for prompt attention. For another thing there was a growing irritation over Bolshevik—shortly Soviet—mendacity on the Continent as well as throughout the Empire, and finally there was the uncertainty and bafflement following inevitably in the wake of *all* recent events.

Asia held a low priority, and, not without corollary, so also in the government's view did Intelligence. All the secret services which had served so well during the war, by late in the 1920s were considered as being less than paramount. That attitude may have been responsible for an embarrassing escapade which occurred in 1921 when preoccupation in other areas precluded the kind of control over the Intelligence community which must always be exercised.

11

Backfire

As early as 1919 there was reason for annoyance with the Russians. Apart from mass murder and a specious ideology, there was clear evidence that they would probably never resolve predicaments at home without resorting to additional murders. This was certainly objectionable, but to many outsiders the dedication to promoting discord, divisions and embarrassment elsewhere, aroused considerable resentment too.

Bolshevism's particular phobia was imperialism. Its earliest demonstrations of this animus were directed towards Great Britain. But there was additionally the re-application of an ancient dictum about dividing friends and allies, such as France and Britain, to augment antagonisms.

Nor did the behaviour of Russians abroad appear inconsistent with the actions of the kind of individuals who now ruled Russia: Lenin, Marx, Trotsky, and eventually Stalin.

The result was antagonism all across Europe, and particularly in London. Restraint was of course endemic, but the basic feeling was still there.

Yet for the Russians there was an irrefutable need. While sowing seeds of dissension on a large scale, and also while the cellars of such places as Lubyanka Prison ran deep with blood from round-the-clock executions, there was an unidealistic fact requiring prompt attention.

Regardless of the degree of insularity the Bolshevik leadership preferred for revolutionary Russia, there had to be trade with other nations.

But Russia had become—and would remain for decades—the largest prison compound, in history. Mistrust was rampant, and while the ultimate compromise for national needs involved trade delegations, for the delegates there was no assurance whatsoever that when they returned they would not be destroyed because of suspicion that they had become contaminated through association.

A huge Intelligence system seemed to be the best answer. Less to spy on outsiders than upon other Russians, and of course since the system did not change—it in fact got worse—the secret services got larger. In time the Russians would literally be ruled by an Intelligence network, but well before that obtained, in 1920–1, their hostility toward Great Britain resulted in a bizarre affair, a sort of backlash which was triggered by the arrival in London, during the month of May in 1920, of a Russian trade delegation, right at the time when Bolshevik anti-British propaganda was especially shrill.

It was asking a great deal of a people who had recently paid over nine hundred thousand lives, and who had in wealth spent more than twice as much as Germany and Austria-Hungary combined— more than all the other Allied countries together, excluding the United States—to defeat the Central Powers, to accept with equanimity the constant derogation and deliberate misinformation being spread about them by Moscow's new leaders.

These were the same people who had failed the Allies at the most crucial time of the war, and who since those days had contributed nothing but discord and opposition towards British efforts to bring order, prosperity and peace back to Europe, Africa and Asia.

Nor did it improve the situation that the trade delegates, under M. Krassin, had an idea that their bargaining position was far more exalted than it was. Then too, the Russians were quick to denounce Britain's anti-Bolshevik pronouncements, some of which had emerged as policy statements, others—more virulent—had emerged as black propaganda from the Intelligence sector.

Then a genuinely magnificent blunder occurred.

Two weeks before the trade conferences were to result in a signed agreement, and unbeknownst to the Foreign Office which had been negotiating with the Russians for a year, another government bureau was producing its answer to Russian disinformation and black propaganda about Great Britain.

On 28 February 1921 the London *Daily Herald* came out with what purported to be a photocopied edition of the Russian newspaper, *Pravda*, in which there was anti-communist black propaganda in the guise of news. However, in accordance with the law, the printer's name in very small print, was given on the last page; it was a London Company, and that was to create quite a sensation.

The *Daily Herald* did not explain how it came by its forged copy of *Pravda*, but as events unfolded and it became known that dozens of copies had been manufactured, the avenues for such an acquisition appeared to be numerous. Maybe the *Daily Herald* should have got its copy much earlier, but in any case the *Herald* was able to sell a lot of newspapers on the strength of an editorial which said in part:

> The title heading of this paper . . . is identical with the ordinary title heading of the Moscow *Pravda*. It states that it is the official organ of the Executive Committee of the Moscow Communist Party, and that it was published in Moscow on Wednesday, September 27, 1921. . . . At the bottom of the back page is the imprint of a London printer. . . . Now how in the world did a firm of London printers come to be printing an imitation of the Moscow *Pravda*? For whom were they printing it?
>
> Investigative reporting turned up some interesting—and embarrassing—answers.
>
> Those imitation *Pravda*s [there was a whole series of them] were produced . . . [by] . . . the London printing firm acting only as printers in the ordinary way of business—by a group of . . . Russian *émigrés*, with the connivance and assistance of the Special Branch at Scotland Yard.
>
> The usual procedure was this: The order for the printing was given by one . . . of the principals of the group of . . . *émigrés*. They . . . paid . . . in cash. . . . Before the paper could be . . . [clandestinely circulated] . . . the imprint must be removed. It was there to comply with the law. . . . No ordinary printer would remove it.
>
> This is where Special Branch comes into the story. . . . There is of course the ordinary printing establishment at the Yard—everyone knows that. But there is also . . . an extra-specially confidential . . . [printing] . . . establishment at Scotland House itself where very private work is done for the Special Branch's own curious requirements, and also on occasion for the Foreign Office and the War Office. . . .

The newspaper went on to say that the commercially-produced forgeries were delivered to Special Branch, and there the printer's name and address were removed, after which the anti-communist forgeries were sent on their way.

The furore was extensive, and the *Daily Herald* was still aiming to sell newspapers when it said: "Who is responsible for employing the men and machines of the British government . . . against the Soviet government?"

Everyone more or less weathered the storm although Prime Minister Lloyd George, the Home Office Secretary, and Director of Intelligence Sir Basil Thomson came in for some direct criticism.

Finally, then, when the trade and amity treaty was prepared in its final draft, a reflection of all that consternation appeared in the part where provisions calling for both Great Britain and the Soviet government to abstain from engaging in black propaganda against one another in the future, was included.

However, aside from fresh interest in such aspects of Intelligence as espionage, counter-espionage, black propaganda, clandestine influence-peddling and electronic eavesdropping, the secret services while certainly languishing since the end of the war, were anything but moribund.

They were not even smaller than they had once been thanks in large part to the number of expatriate groups new in the field, largely White Russians.

Many of these groups established their own anti-Bolshevik organizations in such places as London, Paris and Berlin and throughout the Baltic countries. They spied, acted as terrorists and assassins, produced reams of forged documents, and worked diligently through propaganda to create and maintain as much hostility as possible between Soviet Russia and the West.

Between these groups and the Russian secret services a state of constant war existed, and as long as they murdered and abducted one another few world governments evinced more than a perfunctory concern, but the day when national governments were alone in the Intelligence field had become a thing of the past. At least for the time being.

So muddy in fact did the waters occasionally become that the most expert Intelligence networks were unable to unravel completely several of the major intrigues of those times.

One which had all the elements of falsehood involved an affair which erupted almost simultaneously in the United States and Great Britain, when in 1924 British Intelligence acquired an inflammatory document purporting to be instructions from the Chairman of the Communist International organization—the Comintern —Zinoviev, to the British Communist Party, to "stir up the masses of the proletariat", and to proselytize zealously among Britain's armed services in order to ensure complete paralysis of "all military preparations . . . and make a start of turning the imperialist war into a class war".

The Foreign Office "went public" with this letter. The result, according to Labour Party leader James Ramsay MacDonald, was to cause a defeat for his party, said to be sympathetic to Russia's working class, and, true or not, the Labourites were indeed defeated at the polls, 24 October, 1924.

The Russians heatedly denied authorship of the Zinoviev letter. The acrimony spread to include loyal politicians in Britain as well as many outsiders who were not Russians. It was said, for example, that one of the private *émigré* groups had created a forgery over Zinoviev's signature. It was also alleged that S.I.S. or perhaps Special Branch was responsible, but when the indignation was at its height, after three years of countercharges, on 19 March 1928, following heated day-long debates in the House of Commons, a Labour motion calling for an investigation was defeated by a 326 to 132 votes, and the entire affair was encouraged to fade. But Ramsay MacDonald's parting shot could have contained a mote of truth. He said what was "generally admitted to be a political fraud—a fraud perhaps unmatched in our political history" should not have been swept under the rug.

Subsequently, in Britain, the Zinoviev affair was relegated a niche in Foreign Office history, but clearly the Zinoviev document was an Intelligence product and the question was: which Intelligence bureau, of what country, was responsible?

Historians have to some extent attributed the letter to the Foreign Office's Intelligence Division. They have also picked their way through a maze of seeming contradictions and improprieties which, in government, seem to be endemic. In the end what the Zinoviev letter accomplished may quite possibly have been what it was supposed to accomplish, for although the British government extended *de jure* recognition to the Soviet government in early 1924, all the scattered suspicions and hostilities were crystallized through what was claimed to be a Communist scheme to cause trouble in Britain, as revealed by the Zinoviev letter, and British-Russian relations were to remain to a great degree very cool for almost a full decade. If, then someone did not want a *rapprochement,* they had succeeded.

On the opposite side of the Atlantic reaction to the Zinoviev affair was predictably very loud and bombastic. It followed a tidy little sequence beginning when the Russian Foreign Minister, Georgi Chicherin, approached several travelling United States politicians with a proposal for American recognition of the Soviet government. This occurred in August of 1923.

Following President Coolidge's address to Congress the following December touching upon differences, the Soviet Foreign Minister sent a message to the White House advising that his government was ready to discuss all issues. In response the very elegant United States Secretary of State, Mr Charles Evans Hughes, responded on 18 December in these words:

There would seem to be at this time no reason for negotiations. . . . If the Soviet authorities are ready to restore the confiscated property of American citizens or make effective compensation, they can do so. If the Soviet authorities are ready to repeat their decree repudiating Russia's obligations to this country and appropriately recognize them, they can do so . . . most serious is the continued propaganda to overthrow the institutions of this country. This government can enter into no negotiations until these efforts from Moscow are abandoned.

The Hughes note was given to the newspapers and favourable comment was certain, but the following day, 19 December, the State Department offered another Press release, this time of the "text of instructions given by Zinoviev, President of the Communist International and President of the Petrograd Soviet, to the Workers' Party of America".

These were in part as follows:

The Communist International notes with great satisfaction that the work of the W.P.A. (Workers' Party of America) for the past year has been expressed in a satisfactory broad and real revolutionary work. Particularly pleasing to us is the fact that all dissensions . . . in the ranks of the Party have been liquidated and . . . the advance guard of the revolutionary proletariat . . . will now more successfully conduct its revolutionary work among the millions of American proletarians.

Following this preamble were lists of things to be done to expedite the establishment of Communist supremacy in the United States, none of which was especially remarkable until, at the conclusion, were the words: "We hope that the Party will step by step conquer . . . the proletarian forces of America and in the not distant future will raise the red flag over the White House."

As had happened in England, when the State Department released copies of the Zinoviev message, a predictable storm of denunciation and controversy ensued. Newspapers across the country picked up, repeated, and of course embroidered upon the *New York Times* banner headlines which said: *"Hughes Reveals New Red Orders For Action Here: Zinoviev Tells Workers' Party To Aim At Flying Red Flag On The White House."*

In a private note to President Coolidge, Hughes wrote that "The Department [of State] . . . has a large number of communications with respect to the Russian matter, and evidently, the country is deeply stirred."

There were a small but noticeable number of sceptical communications, too. Several called the 'Instructions' a plain forgery, and in time, as more and more sceptics raised their voices, Charles Evans Hughes ringingly denounced both the sceptics and the Russians, but eventually even people who believed the allegations began to ask for a view of the original Zinoviev letter.

It was never produced. To this date (1979) it has not surfaced. The American politicians were unable to quash so successfully the matter as had the British. They were never able to, even fifty years later when the desire to do so no longer existed; when Zinoviev, Hughes and Calvin Coolidge were dead, and there still has been no original Zinoviev letter produced.

Perhaps because there never was one. Just a copy from British Intelligence.

Soviet Foreign Minister Chicherin, whose earlier efforts to open recognition and treaty talks with the Americans had failed, reacted angrily to what he protested was a "clumsy forgery", and challenged the United States government to produce the original. It was never produced. Instead, additional vituperation masked the United States position, which was about as unenviable as the British position had been.

In the end the attempt to gain United States recognition for the Union of Socialist Soviet Republics failed. Not for another nine years was recognition finally extended. By then, surely, someone's clear design had succeeded very well.

Who, then, produced the Zinoviev documents? Probably not the Russians, who not only wanted recognition, credits and loans, but who desperately needed them all. Further, if Zinoviev had in fact sent forth those instructions, although his leaders could still deny their authenticity, in all probability those denials would have produced a disappearance: Zinoviev's. That did not happen.

What was the extent of American involvement? In a news article from official sources it was said that "the Department of Justice has assured the Department of State of the authenticity of those instructions". How could that have occurred if there were no instructions—unless Mr Hughes, having accepted a British Intelligence signal verbatim, went public on only that basis, and afterwards, with no way out except through bluster, had employed exactly that technique?

British Intelligence was the source of almost all United States *sub rosa* information from Europe. Commonly it was an unimpeachable source, but when the United States asked for permission to scrutinize reports relative to the Zinoviev matter, and other details, from the Soviet Union, British Intelligence courteously declined.

Were the British wholly to blame?

After the March 1917 Revolution, and in the immediately following years, a compact, sophisticated British Intelligence Service had successfully penetrated the Soviet Union all the way to Moscow and the Kremlin, but in the main its spies were Russian *émigrés*. It was known that disenfranchised Russians working hard for the downfall of the Bolsheviks—Menscheviks—all Communists —counted most upon Russia being unable to survive without foreign trade and credit.

There was no goal of these people higher or more desirable than that one.

There was no proof that *émigrés* created the forgeries. Nor in all candour could anyone be expected to produce such proof. Therefore the tantalizing question remains: did British Intelligence, for several obvious reasons, fabricate Zinoviev's letter, or was British Intelligence duped by its own *émigré* secret agents?

One thing appeared quite certain: the Russians were as much in the dark as anyone else. Because they suspected *émigrés* in Latvia were responsible they sent agents from the Foreign Section of Soviet Security Police to Riga. If they ever discovered incriminating evidence it was never passed along; yet, because they had certainly more reasons to debunk British and United States allegations than not to debunk them, it could be assumed that they found nothing.

There the story ends. Almost. Eventually someone may gain access to files which currently are still *verboten*. The truth is certainly available from some source.

For a while it was alleged that the United States Department of State, not British Intelligence, had fabricated the entire affair, and while the possibility certainly exists, there are nuances which encourage a belief that S.I.S. was the originator.

Whoever actually was responsible, whatever the objective, it probably succeeded, for along with delaying British-United States recognition of the Soviet Union, a matter which would naturally discourage loans and trade, suspicion and animosity, already widespread, were certainly fed fresh fuel. There was really nothing else to be gained in the West.

12

A Dying Past—A Discernible Future

Intelligence being the hidden side of a national profile, when after the 1914–18 war it was advocated by those charged with establishing peace and shuffling national boundaries that Great Britain should assume a controlling and pacifying role in the Middle East, secret agents moved in advance of other British elements to assess and evaluate.

Having been there before they were qualified, and yet this area like Europe had moved towards fragmentation; war had made great changes here, in an atmosphere which had rarely throughout an extremely long history been tranquil.

What existed was a quagmire of illogicality, boundaries as illusive as Syrian sand, people steeped in the legends and processes of antiquity, all of it built upon a base of political quicksand composed of two parts unpredictability and one part treachery.

Probably because the idea of empire died hard, especially among the English, as they became masters in this fresh endeavour they administered both as Raj and mandated peace-keeping power.

It worked, although it was always under attack, and if there was any better way none of the army of vociferous denunciators ever proved it. As policemen in Palestine, Trans-Jordan, and Iraq, and already committed in Egypt, Aden and Cyprus, British knowledge-ability abetted a fair—but no nonsense—policy favouring local autonomy where it had any chance at all, force where that had to be provided, and generally an attitude that asked for and received respect without fondness.

It had supporters even among those who resented overlordship in any form. One was the Israeli patriot David Ben-Gurion who joined the army's Jewish Battalion, became a corporal and served in Egypt before being transferred to Palestine.

Years later during the bitter days of Israeli-Arab confrontation, when Israel triumphed she governed Arab territories by the same regulations the British had established a generation earlier.

In a part of the world where boundaries had for centuries turned with the shadows of the sun, the French and British fixed them pretty much as they have remained, and the influence of Europe proved itself more profoundly practical and enduring, despite its relatively short tenure, than the preceding four hundred years of Turkish domination. Although there was inevitable hostility, charges that the British would never depart, that they were carving themselves a third empire, within their hegemony, indications to the contrary abounded including the independence of Yemen, Saudi-Arabia and Persia (Iran), while Israel and Iraq were aided in their nationalist aims, and Egypt—ruled by foreigners for seven hundred years—was repeatedly bolstered with economic aid, military protection and order.

In areas where France held a mandate the emphasis was upon culture and glory. Where the British stood their language was accepted, their commercial and industrial expertise brought economic improvement, their educational system fulfilled dormant hopes, and their superior civil service structure was widely emulated. English common law took firm root in the Middle East.

Aden, where they had built a great military base years earlier, was the fulcrum for their continuing Pax Britannica of a hundred years.

In Egypt where France built the Suez Canal, Britain controlled it. In Iraq where Britain had been established before the war (called Mesopotamia then), she returned in the 1920s to establish order among a dour, fierce conglomerate of Kurds, Sunni and Shia Arabs. Iraq had more built-in headaches for outside administrators than most other Middle Eastern countries.

Britain maintained order, established an adequate kingdom at Baghdad under Feisal, son of Sherif Hussein, sometime ruler of the Hejaz, (the same Feisal the French had expelled from Damascus) and while British policy of enforcing peace was widely respected, it was never a basis for any deeper emotion among a people who had been quarrelling with someone—either alien enemies or among themselves—for five thousand years.

It was the British-created monarchy, advocated by Whitehall as a result of Intelligence assessments, which crystallized the Iraqi resolve for independence, a condition which would remain until the

British withdrawal, after which these endemically cranky people would cheerfully revert. But even then the British influence would linger, strong, equitable, and a part of Iraqi life for many years.

Into the 1940s Great Britain was the force which prevailed from the Turkish border to the South Sudan, from the Mediterranean to Iran. After Britain ousted France from Syria, exiled the pro-German Shah of Iran, and compelled peace in the Holy Land, what had started out less than a generation earlier as a position of mandated authority, an outgrowth of the First World War, had become a third empire. If "a large empire is the best reason for a larger empire", pre-Second World War Great Britain might have established a third one, but while great recovery had followed the First World War, the advent, arrival, and aftermath of the Second World War effectively hamstrung British aspirations in that direction, if they had ever existed.

Britain faded fast, and the sign of her failing power was visible in a domino-sequence: withdrawal from Palestine in 1948, from the Suez Canal Zone in 1954, expulsion of Glubb Pasha from Jordan in 1957, overthrow of the stabilizing British-established Iraqi monarchy in 1958, departure from Aden, 1967, and finally, departure from the Persian Gulf in 1971.

During those hectic years after the First World War up to the chilling early and mid-1930s when a discernible future lay unavoidably ahead, the total success—as well as the occasional failure—of British Middle Eastern policy was based upon an Intelligence capability which had employed a vast secret army of spies; Egyptian spies, Israeli, Iraqi, Iranian, Syrian, even foreign professionals from such organizations as the Russian *émigré* groups, and Germans.

As for British policy during those decades, it only made sense when the struggle between secret Intelligence services which goes on continuously behind all historical events, is understood. But, while the Intelligence purpose preceded the foreign policy of Great Britain, it rarely contributed much to the actual occurrence of events; quite often even foreign policy was no more than a reaction. By the early 1930s, for example, that which in 1918 most leaders had felt confident could not happen again in their lifetimes, had happened. Germany was rearming. The Intelligence networks could confirm this—as they did—and they could offer projections based upon clear facts, but they could not seriously alter events, nor was that their purpose. If it had been, then Intelligence and foreign policy would have merged, something which happened in the United States in the 1960s to everyone's ultimate chagrin. But in Britain the need for separation between those functions had been recognized many years earlier. So what was occurring elsewhere in the world, while Great Britain's main thrust was in the Middle East, although discernible in Whitehall, was not amenable to change at the Intelligence level, nor, as it turned out, was it liable to control at the diplomatic level, whence, if there was to be control or influence the initiative had to come.

Spies in Germany and elsewhere on the Continent shared with those in the Middle East the distinction of facing in the wrong direction. Soviet Russia was the most *visible* enemy, but not the most *deadly*.

Diplomats, on the other hand, with access to broader perspectives, expected danger from yet another quarter, where Japan, a minor consideration in the First World War, was looming as a most serious threat to British interests in Asia and the Pacific.

The militarists, still wearing uniforms requiring swords, were looking in yet another direction. For Britain the blessing of naval supremacy remained paramount until a civilian named Stanley Baldwin had the poor sense to make a ridiculous statement in November 1923: "I think it is well . . . for the man in the street to realize that there is no power on earth that can protect him from being bombed. Whatever people may tell him, the bombers will always get through."

Generals and admirals knew how incorrect such a statement must be. Ten years later Great Britain was ranked sixth or seventh in air power after Russia, Japan, the United States, Italy, France and Germany. (In 1934 Winston Churchill said fifth.)

That same Stanley Baldwin made another prescient pronouncement in the summer of 1934 when he said: "When you think of defence of England you no longer think of the chalk cliffs of Dover, you think of the Rhine. That is where our frontier [now] lies."

But up until that year of 1934 the diplomats, soldiers and the Intelligence bureaux, were facing east towards Communist Russia, the same direction they had been facing from habit since world Bolshevism had been proclaimed.

Two years later Winston Churchill expounded what he held to be the essentials of national survival when he said:

For four hundred years the policy of England has been to oppose the strongest, most aggressive, most dominant power on the Continent and particularly to prevent the Low Countries falling into the hands of such a power . . . we always took the harder course, joined with the less strong power, and thus defeated and frustrated the continental military tyrant whoever he was, whatever nation he led. . . . I know of nothing which has occurred to alter or weaken the justice, wisdom, valour and prudence upon which our ancestors acted. . . . My three main propositions are: First, that we must oppose the would-be dominator or potential aggressor. Secondly, that Germany under its present Nazi regime and with its prodigious armaments so swiftly developing, fills unmistakably that part. Thirdly, that the League of Nations . . . [is] . . . the most effective way to control the would-be aggressor.

Well, an average of two out of three was not bad.

Nevertheless, regardless of solemn warnings, the British pre-occupation in the Middle East, and parallel concern with the Soviet menace on the Continent where it was beginning to appear as a challenge to the 'ancient dictum', overshadowed confirmation of a new German chancellor in 1933, Adolf Hitler. One of the people who certainly contributed to Great Britain's Intelligence war with Russia's growing, far-flung and increasingly proficient secret services was a Russian Jew who had assumed the name of Sidney George Reilly.

There was reason enough for this influence. Sidney Reilly was not just a spy. At the turn of the century he had master-minded, without help, the deliverance of Iran's oilfields to Britain. He was responsible in 1919 for Intelligence briefings of British envoys at the World Peace Conference on the complex Russian situation.

As a member of British Intelligence (I.K.8 section) he collaborated with *émigré* leaders, several of whom, Wrangel, Elvengren, Savinkov (of whom Winston Churchill devoted a chapter in his book *Great Contemporaries*) were high on the Soviet extermination list.

Reilly was, like Boris Savinkov, intensely antagonistic to the systems of both Imperial Russia and Bolshevik Russia. Both Savinkov and Reilly viewed the Czar and Lenin "as the same thing expressed differently", the identical oppression under different names, and they were against what both believed was the world's worst tyranny, and eventually they both earned a similar ending as a result of their uncompromising idealism. But first they served Britain.

Reilly, working through S.I.S.'s chief in Paris (1921–2) Major W.

Field-Robinson, was able to secure monetary support for an assassination plot against Soviet officials travelling to Europe. He owned a forged Russian passport under an assumed name and could therefore presumably, along with co-conspirators Boris Savinkov and Georgi Elvengren, penetrate Soviet security precautions.

But Reilly embarked for New York before the actual attempts were to be made, leaving Elvengren and Savinkov to attempt the killings.

At the time Elvengren and Savinkov were in Paris, Soviet Foreign Minister Georgi Chicherin along with General Verkhovsky, Maxim Gorky and Maxim Litvinov arrived in Berlin. The conspirators hastened to Germany, and never even got close. They were still seeking a way when the Russians entrained for Moscow.

Two years later Elvengren tried again against Chicherin and failed to penetrate Soviet security precautions. This time he had been funded by a Swiss named Ober. The same Swiss lawyer who in 1923 successfully organized the assassination of Soviet Ambassador to Switzerland, Vatslav Vorovsky.

Reilly, meanwhile, working with Sir Paul Dukes, an S.I.S. spy inside the United States, related that he had made up his mind to go into Russia, to press terror attacks against Soviet authorities. He said this to Dukes in 1924. One year earlier he had told his wife Pepita Bobadilla (either his third or fourth wife—and a bigamous wife at that) to "Promise me that whatever happens you will never go to Russia. Even if I write to you asking you to come you must never go." He had no illusions concerning his own fate—or hers, although she was never more than a courier and novice, among professional conspirators.

Nor was he deluded, for although he had served British Intelligence from inside Russia during the late war and had survived, no one knew better than Reilly—and Savinkov—what changes had occurred since 1918. The Soviet secret police were everywhere, they were professional, and they were tireless in their pursuit of people such as Reilly and Savinkov who were high on their liquidation lists.

Why then did Reilly choose to go?

Quite possibly for a number of reasons. One could have been that Winston Churchill, who was not only his friend and upon occasion his confident, but who had also funded him and had faith in him, expected great things from him on a number of occasions. They had exchanged views of what each considered the "arch-enemy of the human race"—Communism.

Reilly may also have felt some disappointment in himself. For all his implacable hatred of Bolshevism, of late he had actually done very little to oppose it.

"If civilisation does not move fast to crush this monster while there is yet time," he wrote, "the monster will finally overwhelm civilisation. . . . At any price this foul obscenity which has been born in Russia must be crushed out of existence. . . . Mankind must unite in a holy alliance against this midnight terror."

That was his sentiment. Yet M.I.5 referred to Reilly as a 'Leftist'.

There could also have been another reason for Reilly's clear feeling of desperation. Of late Britain had begun—finally—to face a different direction. Towards Germany, less towards Communist Russia. Moral support of *émigrés* was still forthcoming but it was cooling, and the funds had dwindled to a trickle.

Commander Ernest Boyce, who had been a chief of British Intelligence inside Russia during the war where he and Sidney Reilly had worked together, was chief of station at Reval in 1925 when secret agents returning from Russia convinced him that as a result of the fierce competition between Leon Trotsky and Josef Stalin over who was to succeed Lenin, Russia was ready for revolution.

At this time, while Reilly was in the United States, it was easy to prove he was not employed by S.I.S. But that was easy to prove any time. A British spy lived and died a British spy. Whether or not the association existed at that time—according to the British it did not—when Reilly received a letter from Commander Boyce, in S.I.S. code, he promptly responded, thus inaugurating a correspondence which continued for months. Boyce needed someone who could penetrate to Moscow, make a sound judgment of the possibility of revolution, and return. No one had better qualifications than Reilly. No one knew better the hazards.

Reilly returned to Europe, met Commander Boyce, accepted the assignment, after which Boyce discreetly returned to London to be clear of any inadvertent fall-out, and Reilly met with several *émigré* friends to discuss his plans. One friend, the White Russian, General Kutyepov who had in the past led raids into Russia, emphatically warned Reilly of "the folly of crossing the border".

Reilly journeyed to Helsinki in Finland, picked up his guides, S.I.S. people, went to Vyborg on the border with Nikolai Bunakov, Commander Boyce's trusted agent and aide, and there met another secret agent, Alexsandr Yakushev, who assured Reilly all preparations had been made and there was no danger. The two of them, Yakushev said, would travel safely all the way to Moscow, and in the event of any awkwardness, Reilly would be under the protection of powerful anti-Communist plotters many of whom were in exalted positions.

Bunakov heard all this before turning back. He had in his possession a letter from Reilly to his wife:

> It is absolutely necessary that I should go for three days to Petrograd and Moscow. I am leaving tonight and will be back Tuesday morning. I want you to know that I would not have undertaken this trip unless it was absolutely essential, and if I was not convinced that there is practically no risk attached to it. . . . If by any chance I should be arrested in Russia, it could only be on some minor, insignificant charge and my new friends are powerful enough to obtain my prompt liberation. . . . My dearest darling, I am doing what I must do. . . . You are in my thoughts always and your love will protect me. God bless you ever and ever. I love you beyond all words.

This letter was never mailed. The following month it was personally handed to Pepita Bobadilla Reilly by Commander Boyce's aide, Nikolai Bunakov who could not speak either Spanish or English, while Pepita Reilly could speak no Russian.

Three versions ultimately surfaced about Sidney Reilly's last assignment. One said that as he was wading across a shallow stream on the U.S.S.R.-Finnish border, either deliberately or accidentally because he was thought to be a contrabandist, he was shot to death by Soviet border guards.

Another version maintained that he did get all the way up to Leningrad, and on Sunday 27 September at the village of Allekul not far from Moscow, travelling in the company of several resistance leaders—OGPU officers to a man—there was a scuffle of some kind and when it was over Sidney Reilly had been killed.

Finally, a defector said several years later that Reilly was arrested and confined to one of the inner-area cells at Lubyanka Prison in Moscow where he was interrogated repeatedly after which he was shot in the back.

Officially, the Soviets made reference to someone named 'Steinberg' being wounded and captured while attempting to slip into Russia from Finland. 'Steinberg' was carrying a forged passport.

After interrogation 'Steinberg' admitted that he was "the notorious British spy, Captain Sidney George Reilly".

Nine months later *Isvestia* ran a lengthy exposé entitled "British Counter-Intelligence at Work", clearly based upon information which almost certainly had been extracted from Reilly, but no mention was made of Reilly's fate.

Many years later, when almost all the principals were dead, a Soviet statement curtly acknowledged that Reilly was "executed on November 5, 1925", which would have been about a week after he crossed the border. No details were given.

Commander Boyce caught some of the fall-out after all. The OGPU had penetrated his network at Reval. It had in fact penetrated to the executive council of Boyce's *émigré* groups and he had been duped right up to the time he innocently, but surely, sent Sidney Reilly to his death. Boyce was demoted and transferred.

Nikolai Bunakov, Boyce's aide, was a double agent. He was subsequently executed by the Soviets, and Alexsandr Yakushev in whom Commander Boyce had put great faith, had been compromised and recruited by the OGPU in April 1922. Since that time for three years, he had been spying not *for* S.I.S. but *on* S.I.S. Eventually, when British Intelligence verified from independent sources that Reilly was dead, it authorized an agent named Shultz—who was actually a very talented spy named Maria Zakharchenko—to notify Reilly's widow. On 15 December 1925 a notice was placed in the London *Times* which said: "REILLY: On the 28th September, killed near the village of Allekul, Russia, by G.R.U. troops. Captain Sidney George Reilly, M.C., late R.A.F., beloved husband of Pepita N. Reilly."

With the departure of this 'master spy', and with the passing of so many like him in the years directly ahead, Kutyepov, Bunakov, Yevgeny Miller, anachronisms lingering long after the Soviet Union was no longer susceptible to internal collapse resulting from outside pressures, went the era of *émigré* counter-terror. For British Intelligence through the late 'Twenties and on into the 'Thirties, a more malevolent peril lay in a different direction.

13

The Phoenix Bird

It probably should have surprised no one that the impossible was in process of re-occurring, that German nationalism was again seeking solace and expression in raw power.

All the world but most pointedly Germany's neighbours had seen this happen time and time again: *Germany* had been defeated, but had the German *army* been defeated?

According to the conclusions of most Germans it had not. German soldiers had been occupying the land of others for several years. No one had done that to Germany. German arms had brushed aside half-a-dozen borders. No German border had been crossed by warring Allied troops, and only five months before the war had ended outnumbered and out-gunned German soldiers had hurled the Allies back to within forty miles of Paris.

None of that appeared as a negative argument. At home Germany had collapsed, but not on the battlefield. The *esprit* had faded long before Compiegne Forest, but the history of German armies suggested that as with their British cousins, they had never been able to quit when they should, and they had stubbornly resisted any perspective, current or historical, which attempted to tarnish their glory with defeat.

Defeat *had* come; it was unpleasant to contemplate it, but there it was. *However*, it had been the result, not of faulty leadership, but rather of poor planning, never lack of skill or ability. In the end when Germany's decimated armies had turned back to march home, their banners still flew and their bands still played. Even then, amidst the terrible hunger and want, the economic and social shambles Wilhelm Hohenzollern had left behind, the revolution, and the reparation demands of former enemies (Germany's soldiers called it a 'stab in the back') they had not given up. They had been betrayed by their allies, not overwhelmed by their enemies.

The Germans had some reason for belief that they had emerged in better condition than most other participants. The German *spirit* at least remained intact. By comparison Russia was a political charnel-house, a social shambles. France had emerged a fatally divided nation. Britain faced rebellion in Ireland and additional difficulties elsewhere, and she was bankrupt. The Americans had gone home to start immediately thinking in terms of what everyone owed them.

Germany alone had returned to the ways of peace, loyalties still intact. She was still willing to think in terms of men and might, and when she was denied military rights, she held secret manoeuvres with the connivance of the Russians.

It was this *spirit* which made Hitler possible for Germany. Germany had been 'betrayed' not conquered, in 1918, and when the appalling post-war inflation was eventually curbed, largely through American grants and loans, when stability guaranteed prosperity, when conditions improved for German workers who had never really, despite some contrary appearances, traded their Teutonic sectarianism for Communist preachments, the spirit was revived.

Elsewhere there had been revulsion at the frightful cost. In Germany 1,773,700 dead were fuel for the fires of revenge, and those who knew Germany, and should perhaps have also therefore known at least what to suspect, were looking in the wrong direction when in April 1920 the German Worker's Party under its latest public relations director A. Hitler, became the National Socialist German Worker's Party, using the abbreviation 'Nazi'.

Europe took note, but not seriously until about 1932, the year before A. Hitler became chancellor of the new Germany. Everyone, it seemed, had enough to do worrying about their own woes. France for example, was trying vainly to surmount one political crisis after another. Britain, her back to an economic wall was resisting to the last breath an inevitable retrenchment, while Italy was, as usual, floundering in an atmosphere not unlike that of an ancient Roman circus.

The Americans, with an entire ocean sea between themselves and Germany, were exclusively concerned with their 1922 World War Foreign Debt Commission. They were busy knocking on the doors of no less than fifteen nations.

United States policy was to collect according to the ability to pay. For an example, while France protested to high heaven, wrung her hands in figurative lamentation and was therefore allowed to repay over a period of sixty-two years at a rate of interest not to exceed one and six-tenths per cent, and Italy was allowed to repay at one and four-tenths of one per cent, according to an agreement reached in June of 1923 Britain, which had already paid more than the others combined, was called upon to repay at a rate of three and four-tenths per cent.

The United States attitude did very little to rekindle affection in Europe where, during the fighting, there had been genuine fondness, for while Americans adopted the position that debts between nations, as with debts between individuals, were matters where repayment was based upon simple honesty, Europeans were less idealistic. The war had devastated their terrain, nearly all the casualties had been theirs, all the devastation, all the expense of rebuilding, had been theirs. Because the war had been a common endeavour with the Allies pooling their resources toward achievement of a mutual salvation and survival, with the United States arriving late and giving mostly material aid while her cities, factories, farms were never harmed so that she could recover almost overnight, her demand for prompt payment of wartime debts rankled.

The richest nation on earth was applying an economic thumbscrew to her recent allies at a time when none of them had had a chance to recover even partially from the most devastating holocaust in history, to that time.

Finally, to further alienate Europeans, when they sought to create a favourable balance of trade in the United States, the Americans countered by erecting tariff barriers.

America's assertion of isolationist disinterest in the affairs of the rest of the world, on into the 'Thirties, had—for the Americans at least—an unforeseen backlash. In Berlin, the Nazi chancellery was immensely pleased.

As for those other lingering aspects of the earlier era, the *émigrés* and the Bolsheviks, they too came into the 'Thirties with an unenviable degree of certainty. For the *émigrés*, the curtain came down with abrupt finality. In 1930 the *émigré* leader, General Alexsandr Kutyepov was abducted on the streets of Paris in broad daylight never to be seen again.

The same thing, with different ramifications also happened to another prominent White Russian, Major-General Nikolai

Skoblin, who was a rarity in Intelligence circles, a triple agent. He was serving British-controlled *émigré* groups, Soviet Intelligence, and later, at about the time of his disappearance, Nazi Germany's 'SD' *(Sicherheitsdienst)*.

The final blow to *émigré* hopes came when General Yevgeny Miller disappeared too, the last of the formidable European White Russians.

General Miller's disappearance was the last abduction, occurring in 1937. He and General Skoblin disappeared simultaneously, with reason to believe Nikolai Vladimirovitch Skoblin's disappearance was more peremptory than planned.

It was on 22 September 1937 that sixty-seven-year-old General Yevgeny Miller handed his aide Paul A. Kussonsky a sealed envelope with the remark that Kussonsky must not believe Miller had gone "out of my mind, but this time I am leaving a sealed message which I ask you to open only in case I do not return".

That was about 10.00 a.m. At 5.00 p.m. when General Miller, a very punctual man had not returned despite an appointment, Kussonsky began to worry. Six hours later he opened the envelope.

Miller's message read:

I have an appointment at 12.30 today with General Skoblin at the corner of Jasmin and Raffet Street. He is to take me to a rendezvous with two German officers. One is a military attaché in a neighbouring country, Strohman, a colonel, the other is Herr Werner, who is attached to the local German Embassy. Both these men speak Russian well. The meeting has been arranged at the initiative of Skoblin. It is possible that this is a trap, and that is why I am leaving this notice.

Yevgeny Miller was never seen again. General Skoblin, on the other hand, suddenly appeared at the modest book store of another *émigré* dishevelled and with an agitated manner, asked for a drink of water, rested briefly, borrowed 200 francs and departed.

Like Yevgeny Miller, Nikolai Skoblin disappeared, leaving behind, among other things, a distraught wife. To this day his fate is unknown. Thirty years later, in 1967, General Miller's wife was still in Paris, waiting.

What significance was attributed to these events? Two facts. Foremost was that Soviet Russia's secret state police had come a long way since 1919. The second consequence was that with their organizations thoroughly penetrated and with their leaders gone, the *émigré* groups were incapable of ever again posing serious problems for the U.S.S.R. which meant that the Russians like everyone else could devote themselves full-time to the greater menace of a unified, rearming Germany. At this time Russia was the only 'Continental' power still placing emphasis on armed strength, aside from Germany.

Even so, and by herself, the Soviet Union was no match for the Germans. Not at least in strategy or spirit, certainly not in proven capability, but in spying she was every bit as good. Better, in fact, but that would not noticeably obtain for another four or five years.

Subsequent historians were to imply this was a result of the victors in 1918 demanding that the German General Staff be disbanded. Since the Intelligence bureaux were an adjunct of the Staff, when the latter was ostensibly dissolved so was the former. Except that neither was actually disbanded. The Staff was reduced in size and responsibility but since there was a home guard, a *Reichswehr*, of 100,000 men there was also a general staff. Not, it was true, with the power approaching that wielded in former times, but the Germans were a very ingenious and resilient people. They could build mountains on nuclei and had been doing so very successfully since Bismarck's day.

As for the Intelligence sector, it became simply the *Abwehr*, meaning 'defence', and its duties revolved around counter-intelligence. There were as many foreign spies in Germany beginning with the 'Thirties as there were anywhere else. British, Polish, Italian, Austrian, French and Russian. It was the obligation of the *Abwehr* to ferret out these people, penetrate their networks if possible, and maintain round-the-clock surveillance. Espionage, or spying on others in foreign countries, while done, was not extensively done. Not in the beginning at any rate, when Nazi Germany's greatest concern was with internal affairs. However there was one exception—code-breaking, and success in this nullified, to a certain extent, the need for German spies in Moscow, London or Paris. If *Abwehr* cryptanalysts could read secret messages emanating from foreign sources, they could equal and probably exceed the value of in-place agents.

The *Abwehr's* chief by 1935 was Admiral Wilhelm Canaris, the same enigmatic individual who was to guide it through most of the stormy years ahead, until he was killed in 1945 and hung naked from a meat hook by the Nazis he had served so well for so long. It was this unique German, operating in Holland, who negotiated with the Dutch and Spanish to build a secret submarine fleet, something

Germany was not supposed to be engaging in at all. He also created the German navy's Intelligence service. He was a professional with principals among Hitler's coarse *Stürmführers*, and eventually it cost him his life.

A corollary condition had also prevailed with the Russians, and it was part of the *Abwehr*'s responsibility to conceal it. The German army, forbidden also to produce warplanes and tanks, agreed to train the huge but clumsy and uninspired Red Army in exchange for the right to produce tanks and war-aircraft within the Soviet Union. Of course the *Abwehr*'s elaborate security was penetrated. By the British, whose spies sent out complete production figures, and also by the host-Russians who were equally certain they would eventually have to fight the Germans—as were the Germans who used Russia's air-space and towns in simulated attacks which, a few years hence, they would return to put into actual effect.

Out of this German-Russian accord came a grim result. Even before Hitler's strike eastward, Russian Intelligence had carefully enumerated the Soviet officers who had worked with the Germans, and suddenly began recalling, and executing them. That was only the beginning of a blood-letting the results of which would be seen later when, under savage attack, the Soviet Union had none of its best military people left.

But for British Intelligence, which had reliable spies throughout the hierarchy of Nazi Germany, the aggravations rarely arose from an inability to procure and forward restricted information. The aggravation, which also plagued French and even Russian spies, was that no action was taken by the home government. Men and women risked their daily lives to uncover secrets for Whitehall which, it seemed, were ignored. This was not the case but it certainly appeared to be.

The truth was that between the spy in Germany, as with the soldier in the field, and those at Downing Street or Whitehall, there existed an almost insurmountable barrier of communication, which an S.I.S. leadership could not explain.

The entire series of events which had been progressing over the preceding decade at a subtly-increasing pace, by 1935–6 had become a headlong rush to make history, and most of the events while vulnerable to good espionage were not influenced by it very much since, for many reasons, the governments which could have halted Hitler, British, French, Russian, American, had no intention of doing so.

Everyone jockeyed for political position, no one chose to risk political death by forcing commerce and industry into an early conscription, warnings of spies notwithstanding. A Soviet-French mutual assistance pact was drawn up in 1935. One year later when it was ratified on 27 May 1936, Hitler's reborn Germany was already moving. A week after ratification, using this treaty as an excuse, Hitler occupied the Rhineland.

That little home-guard *Reichswehr* army had served as an admirable basis for the revival of an entire host of superior organizations, not the least of which was the Great General Staff, and along with this most hallowed of German military institutions came the Intelligence service, full blown by 1936, proving its superiority by the thoroughness of its organizational structuring. Germany's new leaders were men of ability. The new army had to be superior in strategy, tactics, but above all else in its technically advanced capabilities, and these included the secret services, particularly as they pertained to cryptology and counter-espionage, two areas the Germans had discovered, in the decades following the First World War, that the British had excelled in.

They proved themselves technically in advance by creating a successful version of something all Intelligence services had recognized as holding the future of secret communications, a coding and encrypting teleprinter. The German variation was to be known as the 'Enigma Machine'.

14

The Puzzle Within the Enigma

How Germany brought war to the world for the second time in less than a generation has been told and retold. The sudden blows were unprecedentedly swift and terrible: 15 March 1939 Czechoslovakia, 22 March 1939 Lithuania, 1 September 1939 Poland, 9 April 1940 Norway-Denmark, the Netherlands, Luxemburg, Belgium, France. Nation after nation brought down by thrust after thrust from one of the best disciplined war-machines of all time manned by the world's most professional soldiers.

Everything had been either reported as predictable, or it had been put on the line tank for tank, bomber for bomber, submarine for submarine by professional Intelligence analysts. Still, the Germans rolled across Europe as though neither Paris nor London had any idea it could happen. In some high offices it was indeed thought to be a physical impossibility; but never for a moment had the Intelligence services been that deluded.

For a long while they had been reporting from within the Third Reich what had been becoming increasingly evident for more than five years: the New Germany was determined to bring war to the Continent, partly to seek redress of those earlier grievances, and partly because the new *Reichsführer* would not accept any other solution to problems he had for the most part personally manufactured, but whatever the politics or the problems, war arrived, and as had happened before, the Intelligence connection could project, could predict with accuracy, but could neither prevent nor, at first, influence, events.

There was one other Intelligence consideration. With 130 German divisions in the field (French Intelligence said there were only about ninety divisions, a fatal inaccuracy) the problem of communication was critical. Like all else in the new era, communications could not be handled as in that other war. In fact even with as extensive an Intelligence network as the Germans possessed, hundreds of code clerks, complete bureaux of analysts and interpreters, thousands of counter-intelligence people all across Europe, the problem of communication was difficult even within the secret services. But to pass along all the requisite military information was beyond the scope of a room full of code clerks, as in the First World War when it was all done by hand, and that was where the Enigma machine proved as revolutionary in its way as the *Blitzkrieg* concept was in its way. It could mechanically put messages into code faster and more accurately than the best set of clerks in either Berlin or London.

This had been a recognized virtue of code-printers since the first few appeared not very long after the First World War. Another advantage was that clerks did not require extensive training nor acuity.

In the interval between wars at least four machines were invented. One, tested by the hidebound Royal Navy was rejected as too complicated and unreliable, the same terms used to reject a number of other excellent but controversial innovations which outraged naval hideboundedness. This particular machine was capable of entirely doing away with the very cumbersome and vulnerable Royal Navy code volumes, which, as the war progressed, were not only acquired upon several occasions by German sea raiders, but which were stolen with almost monotonous ingenuity by Axis spies and agents.

A code machine eliminated the need for all those secret books. It also cut coding and decoding time to a minimum. The question of credit for the first machine is debatable, but very likely it was invented by a German. Not that who first created a code machine had much effect upon either the conduct or outcome of the war. Otherwise, while in other fields great innovators were able to eventually retire with either honours or riches, occasionally, but rarely, with both, the people who produced those earliest coding machines almost without exception died impoverished and embittered.

A German by the name of Arthur Scherbius made the great Enigma machine. It was an example of the right product at the wrong time. Scherbius's coder came into being shortly after the end of the First World War. No one at that time was interested in buying something whose main purpose was suited to secret warfare.

Roger Casement, the Irish patriot executed for high treason

Harold 'Kim' Philby at a press conference in London in 1955 where he denied involvement in the Burgess-Maclean affair

Guy Burgess the British
Foreign Office official who
spied for the Russians

Donald Maclean and his wife
(*left*) at the cremation service
for Guy Burgess in Moscow
in 1963. Burgess's brother is
on the right

Scherbius tried valiantly, he even organized a modest factory, sold stock, and in 1923 went broke, ended up bankrupt, embittered, and finally died.

Fifteen years later the German War Office picked up Scherbius's enigmatic 'black box' and made it an important part of the design for conquest. Hitler was personally impressed.

Enigma, as with the Japanese Purple machine, consisted of insulated rotary discs half an inch thick and no more than four inches in diameter. Each side of an Enigma disc had twenty-six electrical metal contact points. Each point was connected to another point upon the far side of the code disc by an electrical cord, but these contacts were irregularly spaced to eliminate either too much duplication, or simplicity.

When the plaintext was typed upon an Enigma keyboard, as with a typewriter, the electrical impulse, travelling through a complicated maze, eventually came up with an entirely different letter or number.

When Enigma discs were fixed in place letters could only be substituted for other letters, once. But when discs could be moved, they only had to be turned to an ensuing letter in order to create a new alphabet, or, more correctly a new sequence of letters.

A particular asset of both Enigma and Purple was their versatility. Because the vulnerability of codes was based upon the repetitive use of a particular word or letter or symbol, things which would provide a key to enemy code-breakers, a coding system which had great variation was invaluable.

If an Enigma or any other cryptowriter had as many as four or five rotating discs, the variables were vast. Someone once worked out that a five-disc machine had 11,881,376 available variations.

Letters or numbers engraved upon a coding machine disc determined the category of the message. A 'code' was simply the substitution of one word for another word, while a 'cipher' substituted one letter or numeral for another letter or numeral.

To add fresh dimensions to the nightmares of code-breakers, codes and ciphers were sometimes run together to form a message consisting of jumbled words, letters, and numbers.

Codes were used as a convenient and inexpensive method of communication in both times of peace and war, but ciphers were always secret, and invariably reserved for troubled times. There was no universal interpretation for ciphers as there was, for example, with the Morse Code, for common codes.

General practice had made both designations—codes and ciphers —interchangeable, which technically they were not, but in order to pursue a course of simplicity, and since this is not a technical manual, hereafter, as heretofore, the commonly accepted interchangeable terms will be used.

For the Enigma machine to decode a message, at the receiving station an operator would have no difficulty, providing that the key was known. To baffle someone the transmitting operator had only to revolve his disc a half turn without advising those at the receiving facility.

The British had almost no success in breaking Enigma codes, which of course was the German intention. Probably in time cryptanalysts could have made headway but as mentioned before, a particular advantage in breaking codes in wartime was haste. If a month were required to break the code being used by one of Hitler's *Panzerarmees* in Belgium, the Belgians would have been overrun along with two-thirds of France, and by then the message would probably be *passé* anyway.

British Intelligence, a labyrinth of sophisticated professionalism, had among its options, alternatives and policies, one which was very mundane: 'If you can't beat 'em, join 'em'. If Enigma codes could not be conveniently broken, then join the exclusive club of those who possessed Enigma machines.

A particular advantage for those seeking an Enigma machine lay in the fact that the Germans had built them on an assembly-line basis beginning in about 1938, to be in a position to supply them to all armed force elements, including army, navy, air force services of supply and even negotiating and diplomatic organizations. Although stringent security measures would be in effect, contrived situations being an Intelligence speciality, it was possible a machine could be procured.

As things turned out more than one Enigma was acquired. One was salvaged from a sunken German submarine. Earlier, not long after the Germans began manufacturing the machines, French Intelligence got one, but since secrecy prohibits—even forty years later—detailing how this was accomplished, conjecture suggests that the machine was perhaps stolen part by part by a French spy working in the Enigma factory. When France fell, French Intelligence sent its Enigma machine to London. This was without a doubt

France's most telling blow against Nazi Germany. It certainly was a great contributory factor to the ultimate victory.

S.I.S. may also have bought a machine either shortly after the war began or at roughly the time France fell; a month or so earlier. This is conjecture but there is some corroborating evidence.

Another version mentions a Polish worker being employed in Eastern Germany where Enigmas were being assembled. He understood that what he was working on was some kind of coding machine. After memorizing the parts, he returned to Warsaw, contacted British Intelligence, told what he knew, and after the kind of delay even secret services are not immune to, being bureaucracies, the Pole was smuggled out of the country, given a workshop and told to create an Enigma mock-up in wood, which he did. What S.I.S. wanted to verify was that the Pole was being truthful. His over-sized wooden machine was a very good prototype of what the Germans called their 'Enigma' machine. Sir Hugh Sinclair, Chief of S.I.S.—who was to die shortly and be succeeded by his subordinate, Colonel Stewart (later General) Menzies—authorized Commander Alistair Denniston, a cryptanalyst in Room 40 during the First World War, later head of the Code and Cypher School, to inconspicuously visit Poland and confer with Polish Intelligence.

The upshot of this meeting was that Polish Intelligence, supplied with funds by Britain, would attempt through its spies in Germany to acquire an Enigma machine intact and operable.

How they managed this achievement was a spectacular race against time; the Germans were already massing on the Polish border.

This affair was the ultimate secret. All the major communications of Hitler's superb war-machine were to be transmitted by Enigma, and they were indeed a superior means of secret communication.

The Poles got an Enigma, delivered it to Alistair Denniston, and his dramatic accomplishment of delivering it to London in utmost secrecy, even within the secret services, was a spectacular achievement.

The old Greek word for puzzle, 'Enigma', was henceforth to be far less of a puzzle to Germany's enemies in high positions than Hitler's Intelligence people thought. The loss of only one of their Enigma cryptowriters was to most certainly alter the course of the second great war of the twentieth century.

That first Enigma machine to fall into British hands was battery operated and compact. It resembled a conventional typewriter. When letters were activated on the keyboard, electrical impulses began their complicated run to the discs, a panel of small light-bulbs glowed to facilitate coding even in the dark, and an appropriate letter appeared.

S.I.S. began to organize a special branch to handle Enigma— termed the Ultra Secret, or just plain 'Ultra'. Some of Britain's best mathematicians were drafted, along with knowledgeable cryptanalysts. One member of the Ultra team, Group Captain F. W. Winterbotham wrote *The Ultra Secret* (Harper and Row, 1974) presenting in considerable detail many aspects which were still classified top-secret in 1974.

The Ultra team was sent to the countryside, away from attack-prone London, with their machine, were installed in a roomy residence at Bletchley in the South Midlands, and there went to work familiarizing themselves with Enigma and its variations, its temperament, and mechanical idiosyncrasies. As time passed other machines were acquired. Some, it was said, were faithfully duplicated by British master machinists.

One of the amazing facts to come out of the entire Enigma affair was how perfectly the secret of its existence in Britain was kept from the Germans, and also from all but a very select group of others, including the Americans, as well as other British defence departments.

But Enigma could still have proven a source of exasperation if another electrical discovery had not appeared at a time when practically limitless variations of Enigma codes were being studied at Bletchley, The computer. This second electronic device could convert Enigma's variables in moments, was capable of breaking down hordes of calculations in minutes. The first coded Enigma message from the Germans required more than a month of intense cryptanalytical work to break by the Ultra team at Bletchley. A computer could compare, discard, locate, accept and accurately print out in moments.

Thus it became possible for British Intelligence to read German military orders and plans without knowing in advance the particular key to a secret coding. Nothing was to affect the outcome of the Second World War so dramatically.

15

How to Lose while Winning

The Ultra project was to eventually create sufficient public impression to bring Intelligence work out of the closet. That would not be the case for a number of years after the Second World War. However, when it did eventually obtain, public enlightenment respecting the function of Intelligence would help to place the secret labour of a great many talented and courageous people in proper perspective, something entrenched secrecy had prohibited for centuries.

But most certainly secrecy was inherently what Intelligence work could not survive without. Where it began to be a disservice was when it became an Intelligence fetish. Secrets from Walsingham's day remain secrets today, four hundred years later.

Ultra's incredible success was in large part due to Group Captain Winterbotham, who knew the value of what he controlled. He realized for example that if Allied commanders were furnished with secret German plans which enabled them to circumvent German aspirations and to defeat German forces, within a short space of time the Germans would surmise their Enigma signals were being read in England, and that, obviously, would lead them to scrap Enigma and produce something else. This conceivably could have very grave consequences for the British who were at this time facing the might of Germany practically alone, and needed every variety of help they could get.

Captain Winterbotham devised a plan whereby only the top people got copies of Ultra translations. These were not to be passed around, and all precautions were to be taken to provide sound cover for the Ultra project. Where possible, conventional espionage sources were to be credited with Ultra information.

The most unbelievable aspect of this was that it worked. From 1940 until the war's end some five years later the Ultra project consistently provided, first the British and French, and ultimately the Americans and others, with absolutely genuine and reliable German orders, summaries and plans.

The remarkable fact was that during all those years, and despite having German spies in Britain, some presumably in sensitive positions, the secret was kept. As for that other 'ally' the Soviet Union, it probably knew of the Ultra project through some highly-placed spy such as 'Kim' Philby who admittedly supplied the Russians with military and political secrets from the early stages of the war until he was removed as a high official of the British Intelligence Service in 1951.

There would have been no reason for the Soviets to signal Nazi Germany about an Intelligence matter even before Hitler's 1941 invasion; afterwards there was every reason not to, so if they knew of the Ultra project or that the British had acquired an Enigma machine, clearly, and for whatever reason, they kept the secret.

The first Enigma reports dealt with what certainly would have been very disheartening information had it been widely disseminated. It gave in piecemeal detail what in total added up to the German 'battle order', or strength, disposition and armament of all German armed power. It was such an overwhelming array of raw might that the infinitely weaker British could not possibly prevail against it. But as with the bumble-bee whose wingspan could not support his weight or body size in flight, but who went ahead and flew anyway because he did not know he could not fly, the British never stopped fighting.

And yet they learned a bitter lesson, for while they knew exactly where the panzer groups were, where the aerial attacks were to take place and which army corps were racing across Europe, they could do almost nothing about any of it, and this was an Intelligence lesson which was to be driven home time and time again in the years ahead. The best Intelligence could be no more effective than a nation's leadership would permit it to be. If in the preceding years, government had elected not to prepare for war despite all the reliable Intelligence information proving that there was absolutely no alternative, then the clearest consciences and the most bitter hearts could be found in the Intelligence services.

An example of how Ultra helped Britain win while losing occurred on 23 April 1940 when the renowned German Field-Marshal von Brauchitsch issued orders for a continuation of "the encircling movement" against Britain's Expeditionary Force (B.E.F.) in France "with the utmost vigour". When the Ultra interpretation of this order was placed in Prime Minister Churchill's hands, he ordered that the B.E.F. be pulled back to the beaches at Dunkirk in all haste. The rest became stirring history. A fleet of little boats crossed over to aid in the evacuation, the B.E.F. was saved—not without a frightful cost—and Winston Churchill became the Ultra project's most formidable mentor.

Three months later *Reichsmarschall* Goering signalled his *Luftwaffe* commanders to prepare for the invasion of Britain. This time when the Enigma translation was placed before the Prime Minister his reaction was immediate and fierce. Britain he exclaimed would if necessary fight the Germans on the beaches and in the streets.

The invasion did not materialize although preparations were completed right down to the ranks of tethered barges along the French coast. But the 'softening-up campaign' got under way. It evolved into the aerial engagement known as the 'Battle of Britain' and *Reichsmarschall* Herman Goering was so certain his *Luftwaffe* could break Britain's back and compel capitulation without naval help that he evidently convinced Hitler. (There may have been even earlier sympathy with the idea. German generals had no experience crossing seas, and no training in that area. Hitler was personally terrified of anything larger than a narrow river.)

Goering's coded messages, picked up and translated at Bletchley, were passed along at only the highest levels and now Britain was to learn how superb her Intelligence services were, and how inadequate she was in other fields.

Especially frustrating was the Enigma information which gave locations of German airfields in France, and the details of which *Luftflotte* groups would be based there, all of it tantalizingly revealing to R.A.F. bomber commands, who dared not risk any losses.

The sequence was roughly to follow a pattern established back in Berlin. In April the B.E.F. was to have been either captured or destroyed. In May and June the invasion was to be prepared for, (it was called Sea Lion). In June and July the German Air Force was to bomb Britain to her knees. In August the Channel invasion was to be undertaken, in conjunction with a great airlift of German troops, equipment and supplies.

Enigma's messages proliferated at each stage, right up to the aerial campaign, and Goering's—or someone's at any rate—fatal mistake was confidently to overlook what Adolf Hitler had long known—British resistance even under overwhelming adversity, could not be overcome from the air. Conversely, Winston Churchill's absolute faith in Britain's warships and their ability to turn back or sink Hitler's invasion craft was equally vulnerable. Germany had command of the skies. The English Channel was no more than a large pond. The best warships could not manoeuvre quickly enough to avoid aerial bombs dropped from squadrons of overhead aircraft.

The result of the Battle of Britain proved Hitler more nearly correct, and the Ultra project helped greatly, but certainly of equal, perhaps even greater value, were the Air Force's own early warning coastal systems, as well as reports from S.O.E. agents (Special Operations Executive) and other secret service personnel on the Continent, where every German activity was spied upon and reported.

The odds in aircraft superiority against Britain were thought to be about 3–1. The British discovered, beginning 12 August when Air Marshal Goering's 'Operation Eagle' began, that for all its vaunted superiority, the *Luftwaffe* was susceptible to radar early detection, good groundfire, and the unexcelled valour of the men who flew Britain's Spitfire and Hurricane warplanes. On 15 August *Luftwaffe* aircraft, up to two hundred and seventy, came over to bomb. Ultra signals plus radar reception had provided early warning; the problem of defence arose quite simply from the fact that the Royal Air Force did not have enough aircraft to effect a total interception.

German losses were disproportionately great, because, according to knowledgeable air officers, German fighter aircraft did not have a fuel capacity which would allow them to provide protection for the more vulnerable bombers, over and back. Whatever the reason, Goering's bombers were paying a high toll, and Britain's diminishing fighter aircraft had to be sent aloft only upon special occasions.

Those whose duties had to do with anticipating each German attack had to bitterly stand by and watch wave after wave of enemy bombers wing in from France, Belgium, Holland and Denmark to devastate British towns, cities and aerodromes, as well as army and navy facilities. Intelligence had never been able to provide a better example of how it could not, under some circumstances, affect events beyond predicting that they would occur.

The story of Britain's survival against Germany's aerial on-slaught became an epic of heroic resistance which would be graphically told down the long decades after peace returned. For the Intelligence people it was a long moment of low tide and desperation, then on 7 September, came the message that Operation Sea Lion was to be undertaken, preceded, so it was assumed, by air-lifts of German troops as well as air-drops of parachutists.

The Royal Air Force had thus far been able to avoid being pulled into German traps, thanks in great measure to the cryptanalysts attached to the Ultra project. Now, if the Enigma signals were traps, then they would be the first, and since it seemed unlikely that they were, the R.A.F. went after those invasion barges across the Channel, striking at night in order to minimize risk.

That same night German bombers came in from the Continent, more than two hundred of them. The R.A.F. had been alerted well in advance. It went out to meet the Germans before they got close, and while some got through many did not.

Those barges were still across the Channel. Inclement weather kept them there, but so also did a lessening degree of enthusiasm among the Germans for an across-Channel invasion.

On Sunday 15 September German bombers came again, great numbers of them, and British strategy, based upon inferences direct from Enigma communications, encouraged Britain's Air Marshal Hugh Caswell Dowding to seize upon this moment to send aloft everything which was available.

There were almost a thousand German aircraft, and seven hundred of them were fighters to protect the bombers. Air Marshal Dowding timed his strike expertly. Seventeen squadrons of R.A.F. aircraft rose to the attack. German Intelligence had reported no-where nearly that many serviceable aircraft in Britain.

But that was not all. When the fighter aircraft compelled the Germans to turn tail and run for it, another four squadrons were waiting near the coast.

Later, Air Marshal Goering made a second and final effort. This time almost twenty R.A.F. squadrons met his aircraft and as before the Germans had to turn back. This marked the end of Hitler's plan to soften Britain up for his sea-borne invasion. Being late in the year it also coincided with the beginning of bad weather in the Channel. Operation Sea Lion, as well as its aerial counterpart Operation Eagle, were finished.

But the after-shocks lingered. The terrible battering Britain took from Goering's bombers stunned the world. The civilian toll in such places as London and Coventry aroused considerable antagonism towards Germany throughout the Americas, throughout all the committed and uncommitted nations which had watched.

The Intelligence services drew some satisfaction from their part in the victory, which at that time appeared shaky for no one could be certain the Germans might not mount another aerial effort. But shortly thereafter, events in another area of the world demonstrated how the two basics of modern Intelligence work, innovative, peripatetic human spies, and versatile electronic communications, in this case the Enigma machine, when employed simultaneously could do something Goering's *Luftwaffe* had been unable to do; soften up the enemy.

A directive from *Reichsführer* Hitler ordering German forces in the Balkans to move toward Greece indicated that the Germans, unsure of their Italian allies, proposed to protect their southern flank against the British forces in the Middle East by another invasion. Churchill's response to this directive was to propose strengthening the Greeks by taking some of the British forces from Sir Archibald Wavell's Middle East Command, which was already an extremely 'thin red line'.

Churchill's strategy made that 'red line' even thinner. Nor was it to be successful at stopping Hitler's thrust towards Greece, but it most certainly abetted a series of demoralizing events which were shortly to take place in Africa.

In February Enigma reported that the Swabian, General Erwin Rommel was to be in command of a German army, the *Deutsches Afrika Korps*, shortly to be sent to Africa. This was to consist of the 15th Panzer Division and the 5th Light Motorized Division both of which were to be in Africa by May. Not only was General Wavell's thinned-down command to be challenged, but Britain was now to face the German war machine on two fronts, a situation which was destined to put an insurmountable strain upon Wavell's 'desert rats'.

The Enigma messages subsequent to Rommel's arrival in Africa, and his assumption of command, convinced British commanders that Wavell's condition left just one available option—strategic withdrawal, back in the direction of Egypt from whence he had come.

Rommel was a superb tactician. It helped too that the British forces had already opted for a withdrawal, and while this was demoralizing for the B.E.F. it was largely responsible for Rommel's initial successes and the high morale of his forces.

But—this was not entirely a campaign of troops and motorized units. It was also a campaign of supplies and the ability of suppliers to deliver them. Africa unlike conquered Europe, possessed no great industrial areas. Everything from tyres and tank treads to ammunition and food had to be put down from ships which crossed the Mediterranean Sea, quite a few of them arriving from such distant ports as those of the Baltic and the North Atlantic.

Rommel's pace was swift; it required great amounts of fuel, spare parts and tyres, but mostly fuel. The Enigma signals to Field-Marshal Albert Kesselring, Rommel's immediate superior, were constant and unchanging, he needed supplies desperately. Without spare parts for the tanks and trucks, the reconnaissance and support vehicles, he could not persevere.

Ultra project personnel passed along every interception between the German commanders, and eventually, as supplies for Rommel appeared to be going elsewhere it was not difficult, reading additional interceptions, to figure out that Hitler's long-expected assault upon the Soviet Union was being readied at the expense of other German elements such as Rommel's *Afrika Korps*.

Finally, then, there appeared a particular secret agent. His code-name was 'Robin'. It is still the only name used in referring to him. He was a Swiss-French merchant of Jewish descent who had served as a British spy since 1940. He did not accept pay. Being a man of independent wealth he operated entirely at his own expense.

This man under the name 'Herr Walter' made the acquaintance of a civilian at a party given in occupied Paris by Russians. The stranger was clearly German and despite civilian attire was a soldier. 'Herr Walter' and the German left the party and in the German's chauffeur-driven car made the rounds of Paris bistros, and because the German was a hard drinker before too long he had to be returned to his hotel by Herr Walter and the German chauffeur.

The chauffeur was an SS non-commissioned officer. His inebriated employer was a *Standartenführer* (Colonel) of Reich Minister Albert Speer, chief of German war production.

Night after night Herr Walter and the Colonel prowled Paris.

Usually, the partying ended when the Colonel became too drunk to navigate. Then Herr Walter would take him back to his hotel, roll him into bed, then search among the German's papers for documents marked *Geheime* (secret) or *Streng Geheime* (very secret). Later, at his own hotel 'Robin' prepared transmissions of duplicated material for London. In October 1942 the Colonel's papers yielded a special bit of information. General Rommel's complaints of chronic shortages since early 1941 were to be corrected by top-priority shipments of fuel and spare parts from French ports.

At this time Wavell's successor in Africa, British Lieutenant-General Montgomery was poised with his Eighth Army to press a vigorous attack, and General Rommel, recently returned from sick leave in Germany, was prepared to resist. It was of crucial importance that adequate supplies reach Rommel in time for him to halt the British.

According to information forwarded by 'Robin' an Italian convoy outward bound for Benghazi laden with Rommel's desperately needed parts and fuel was to depart about the third week in October.

In the last week of October, while Montgomery's army and the *Afrika Korps* were engaged in battle, British aircraft located the Benghazi-bound convoy and attacked it.

Most of Rommel's parts and fuel went to the bottom of the Mediterranean. What remained of the convoy was scattered and Rommel's panzers, useless without parts and fuel, could not maintain the German line. General Rommel undertook the retreat out of Egypt which "culminated on the 12th November with the area being back under Allied control".

A few days earlier, on 8 November 1942, a combined British-American force landed in Africa in what was the largest amphibious operation in history—850 ships in all categories, and from that date forward the *Afrika Korps* continued to lose ground.

In Paris, 'Robin' had meanwhile made another startling discovery —one which was at the root of *Reichminister* Speer's engineering aide being in France. Germany had perfected its *Vergeltung-swaffen* (Revenge Weapon), the notorious 'flying bomb' called a 'V-1', which was to create such indiscriminate havoc in Britain. 'Robin's' hard-drinking German Colonel was to make preparations along France's northern coastal areas for the construction of launching sites. This information proved invaluable. British aircraft repeatedly struck at those launching sites in the months ahead, although a really adequate defence against 'buzz-bombs' was never discovered.

The main purpose for the German colonel's presence in Paris, when it was discovered and reported to S.I.S., turned out to be a fringe benefit in relation to what else 'Robin' had been able to glean. It also emphasized the importance of what Napoleon had said about one spy in the right place being worth twenty thousand men on the battlefield.

16

The Secret Struggle

Ultra, in a sense, could have been compared to 'open' Intelligence, the accumulation of information about an enemy derived from censored dispatches, newspapers, radio broadcasts et cetera. It was different from reconnaissance, battlefield, or interrogatory Intelligence in that the other varieties could be used—and invariably were—to verify one another. With Ultra the nature of the project to a considerable extent inhibited this. In fact some of the coded messages to General Rommel, as an example, were intercepted and read before they reached him, and were therefore not subject to prompt verification.

In the case of field orders, it was common among Intelligence services to take precautionary action until a projected event actually took place. Suspicion was built in. Every day, somewhere, misleading information—*dis*information—was being fed by the ream into espionage networks to be passed along, the result not infrequently amounting to an ambush.

Among the Americans, when they finally arrived in Europe, there was scepticism, probably justified, about Ultra's unimpeachability. At a very early briefing a tough American general, a deputy under General Dwight Eisenhower, Mark Wayne Clark, listened to a briefing on Ultra, arose and stalked out, unwilling to believe that anything as comprehensive had existed for so long without being compromised. It would have been simple to convince him through past examples, but it also happened to be very easy to manufacture any kind of propaganda out of events with which everyone was familiar.

Winston Churchill had confided in United States President Franklin Roosevelt that he had a "most secret source" of Intelligence. From that point on, as the Americans became increasingly operational in all areas, they were accepted into the exclusive Ultra

'club' according to the same requirements of absolute confidentiality which prevailed with the British. While there could have
been reason to worry, the Americans being garrulous by nature if
their history was any indication, the Ultra secret proved to be completely safe with them.

Among the Allies there was still another nation which was concerned with Enigma. Adolf Hitler's savage assault on the Soviet
Union in midsummer 1941 provided the British with sound
evidence that the Russians had mastered Germany's secret communication system. S.I.S. verified this discovery through monitoring transmissions between Occupied Europe and Moscow.

The war had four years yet to go when Germany invaded Russia,
and by this irresponsible move, based upon the most incredibly
incorrect Intelligence, *Reichsführer* Hitler had forfeited Germany's hope of victory. No single nation on earth including the
largest in terms of territory, the Soviet Union, or the largest in terms
of population, China, could have succeeded in what Hitler was
trying to do with Nazi Germany.

But for several years successive hammer blows by Germany's
foes did little more than rebound from Hitler's armour, so superbly
trained were his fighting forces; then the wearing down began. By
1943 stalemates were occurring and by 1944 reverses were unavoidable. The winding down began very gradually as the over-extended
fighting machine lost headway. Although the war would be won in
Europe, in Asia and the Pacific over vaster expanses of terrain
Imperial Japan, another member of Germany's Axis, (along with
Italy, Hungary, Finland, Bulgaria, Austria and Rumania) had
initially made great strides in her war of conquest, only to begin
losing momentum also when the *real* situation began to replace the
imaginary situation, the way Japan's Warlords had incorrectly seen
it when they first overran British colonies and American possessions. The Allies *could* wage a two-ocean war, one while facing
west, one while facing east, but it required great sacrifice, and much
time, to prove it, and meanwhile the Japanese and their 'co-
prosperity sphere' figured very prominently in the lives of everyone
within the areas bounded by the Bering Strait, the Antipodes
Island south of New Zealand, the Yangtze River in the East and the
Colorado River to the West.

American Intelligence had for some time used the code-word
'Orange' in reference to the Japanese. No doubt from that

beginning Japanese codes were given names such as 'Red', which referred to an early code, and finally, after Pearl Harbour and the bitter-deadly island-hopping war which followed, they called Japan's encoding machine 'Purple'. The Japanese called the same machine '97-shiki O-bun In-ji-ki. (Roughly translated this meant 'Alphabetical Typewriter 2597', the number signifying the year of the Japanese calendar Purple machines were first used. The 2597 corresponded to the West's calendar year of 1937.)

For the Americans, breaking the Purple machine's secret was to prove the most arduous undertaking their secret service crypt-analysts had tackled. By the time Japan and the United States were locked in combat William Friedman's black chamber had grown considerably, and along with it the United States established competent army and navy Intelligence bureaux. Because the war with Japan was predominately a naval conflict United States Navy Intelligence personnel were to handle the bulk of interceptions but it was Friedman's Army Signal Intelligence Service which eventually, after twenty months of unceasing effort, broke the Purple codes. Friedman's triumph caused him to suffer a nervous breakdown.

How the Japanese perfected their coding machine was the subject of at least three different explanations. One story had it that a prototype was captured when a British far-eastern possession was overrun very early in the war. Another inference suggested that the Japanese created a machine without benefit of outside influence to suit their particular requirement, and again a very reasonable explanation had to do with the acquisition of a German Enigma machine, without German knowledge, from which was created the first Purple machine.

One thing was obvious. Any Japanese machine had to be built around a very unique language. For British and United States Intelligence people the work of breaking Purple codes was made more arduous by the difficulties inherent in a language which was generally incomprehensible to Westerners.

But clearly, Japanese confidence was great. Even before the 7 December 1941 attack on Pearl Harbour they were busily transmitting all kinds of messages over their Purples. However, during the actual attack on Pearl Harbour, between the time of arrival in the strike-zone and the time of assault, they maintained radio silence, a fact which led to erroneous conclusions in some quarters that they suspected their codes had been broken—which they had—

Oleg Penkovskiy grips the rail of the dock as he is sentenced to death for spying for British Intelligence

George Blake arriving back in Britain after being held by the Communists
in Korea. He was later sentenced as a Russian spy

but the real reason for radio silence had to do with the knowledge that, even in those days, an enemy could be located *by the sound* of radio transmission. It was not necessary to understand a code or even a language. As long as someone operated radio equipment, detection devices could pinpoint his location.

However, radio silence was only part of the reason the Japanese avoided early detection at Pearl Harbour. The major cause had to do with United States incompetence at the Intelligence level. United States counter-intelligence had been monitoring Purple transmissions for at least a year prior to the Pearl Harbour attack, and had abundant evidence that an attack was coming, yet almost nothing was done.

As for the machine, it not only resembled the German Enigma it also operated according to the Enigma principles, but then so did most other cryptowriters including those in use by British Intelligence, and the other, 'Convertor M209', used by the Americans, which had been perfected, but not invented, by a Russian-born Swedish citizen named Boris C. W. Hagelin.

The Purple Machine, as with Enigma, employed four discs. Hagelin's Convertor M209 used six discs with a 'safe factor' of 101,405,850 variations before beginning to repeat. Purple, minus two discs, in comparison, had a diminished safety factor which was a handicap only providing that a jumbling process was overlooked, which it would not be, especially during wartime.

Basically Purple, like Enigma, changed an intelligible plaintext message into a coded message, when the operator typed out his legible transmission upon one machine and it was electronically transferred to a grid of letters or symbols from where the electric impulse passed along to a second machine, which typed out the code-letters. In reverse, *de*ciphering was accomplished with the same facility.

In breaking a Purple code—apart from having to know the Japanese language, a feat in itself among Westerners—it was essential that the formula which governed selections through the encrypting grid be broken down. One way to accomplish that was by maintaining a vigil over all events which would most probably require comment, then, using key words from newspaper or radio broadcasts, work out their equivalents through—often repetitious—coded letters or symbols.

During the war in Europe the British successfully employed a practical variation of this system. Unable to break a particular code but intuitively certain a specific transmission implied 'tanks', a number of these vehicles were moved up, they waited, and when coded warnings went out to German field units the two words matched, a key was established, and the code was broken.

Another example occurred in 1942 when Japanese Fleet Admiral Isoroku Yamamoto had secret orders transmitted by Purple machine to all units of Japan's navy. At Pearl Harbour, United States cryptanalysts of Naval Intelligence intercepted the message, (in code 25 Japanese Navy) and worked their way towards a solution which at considerable length explained how part of Japan's fleet was to create a diversion in the Bering Sea, and while part of the United States Pacific fleet steamed north, the Imperial Navy would strike at Midway Island.

JN25 was not completely decipherable, so the crucial designation (AF) of the area to be assaulted was not known until tabulators dropped reference cards which showed that Japanese pilots passing within sight of Midway Island had referred to their position as being over 'AF'.

Still, United States Commander of the Pacific Fleet, Admiral Nimitz, required verification. Naval Intelligence had a bogus message transmitted from Midway in a code known to have been broken by Japanese Intelligence. Dutifully, the Japanese made the interception and re-transmitted the message to area warships as having emanated from 'AF'. Admiral Nimitz ordered the full force of his fleet to Midway, and not only arrived before Admiral Yamamoto expected him, but came in full force. What has since been called one of the "most decisive battles of history", resulted in a crushing defeat for the Japanese Navy. The four great aircraft carriers from which had been launched the aircraft which attacked Pearl Harbour, were sunk. Japan's losses in men and ships were great and irreplaceable. The Battle of Midway, which Admiral Chester Nimitz called "essentially a victory of Intelligence", doomed Japan's chances for sea mastery in a war which was entirely sea-oriented.

Other battles with similar but less spectacular outcomes were to follow United States-British co-operation in the Intelligence field throughout the Pacific Theatre. S.I.S., which had earlier mastered the basics of coding machines, built a simulated Purple machine. The Americans also built one but their most successful means of interception was provided when they captured a Purple intact.

It was from this beginning that Allied Intelligence finally began to equal that of the Japanese, and to eventually surpass it with the result that for the Japanese the war began to go badly.

British-United States interceptions were code-named 'Magic'. Information prefaced with that designation was entitled to priority. One particular 'Magic' message resulted in the death of Japan's renowned Fleet Commander, Admiral Yamamoto, architect and final authority of the Pearl Harbour attack, a man of great power and prestige and one of Japan's most esteemed *Samurai*.

Yamamoto, who had been elated at the success of Nippon's superior Intelligence capability in 1941, which had enabled Japan seriously to damage United States power at Pearl Harbour, was still relying heavily on Intelligence two years later, when he became a victim of it.

An intercepted Purple message indicated that he was to inspect personally a number of Pacific outposts from which the Japanese were shortly to launch a series of co-ordinated air and naval attacks against American positions among the Solomon Islands.

Yamamoto was to fly by bomber to the island of Bougainville on 18 April 1943. This information was passed to the Air Corps Command at Henderson Field on the island of Savo. On the eighteenth, P-38 fighter aircraft went aloft, made the interception, shot Yamamoto's bomber out of the sky killing all on board including the Japanese Fleet Admiral, who was found dead inside the wreckage in a sitting position leaning upon his sword. Not a single American aircraft was lost.

The year 1943 was the beginning of a long count-down for the Axis allies in Europe. Reverses and stalemates were followed, ten months after Isoroku Yamamoto's passing, by the D-Day invasion of Hitler's *Festung Europa*.

In late summer 1944 when Hitler sent one of his rare Enigma messages, commanding his marshals to launch an attack and divide the oncoming Americans near Clerbourge, the Ultra group swiftly relayed these orders with a fatal result. Three Allied armies caught the Germans on the flank. The German commander, Gunther von Kluge reported by Enigma to Hitler that Germany's assault had been stopped "with the loss of over half the tanks".

Germany's dogged resolve, as in the First World War, kept the *Feldgrau* fighting until May 1945, another three months. The

Japanese did not yield until September 1945 when two atomic bombs, the creation of a joint United States-British scientific effort, ended Japanese resistance almost overnight.

The Second World War was finished.

17

The Bona Fides

There is evidence that in Germany as Hitler's personal irrationality became more manifest, and violent, much reliable but unpleasant information was withheld from him. For example an accurate analysis concerning the consequences of an attack upon the Soviet Union was available months before Germany invaded Russia. It was withheld.

The Great General Staff, like Adolf Hitler, was confident of a swift victory. German Intelligence had evidence to the contrary. At the height of the war in Germany a negative attitude was comparable to treason, and a common punishment for treason was a bullet in the back of the head—*Genichschuss*.

How much Intelligence was withheld, and what the consequences amounted to were—and still are—matters of conjecture. But there was one fact neither Hitler nor the Great General Staff appreciated right up to the end—the extent of foreign—mainly Russian—penetration of Germany's military, diplomatic and internal political structures.

The same held true of Japan. Before the war ended, successful spies of the calibre of double-agent Richard Sorge (eventually beheaded for being a Soviet spy) operated successfully throughout Japan and her conquered territories. However the most successful penetrations did not occur until the last months of the war, and after, when, in the period of demoralization, confusion and uncertainty, which followed defeat, secret agents appeared in considerable numbers, and had little difficulty infiltrating every phase of Japanese life.

After the First World War all war-oriented facilities had atrophied. At the conclusion of the Second World War an unprecedented and world-wide espionage assault was launched by the Soviet Union, and to a considerable extent that precluded cut-backs

in some war-related areas, a situation which was to cause a continuation of war-like expenses, something recovery and prosperity
could live with, only in an inflationary environment.

Intelligence filled the void left by demobbed armies and navies.
Actual armies of spies existed. Every capital of Europe housed
hosts of spies and counter-spies. Eventually West Germany had a
larger espionage community than any other Continental nation. At
one time Berlin had more C.I.A. agents than Washington.

This secret war was undeniably a continuation of the overt war
but with a fresh alignment of enemies, a truly world-wide theatre of
operations, and rules the Western nations were most certainly
ignorant of for the next ten or fifteen years. It was another variety of
Blitzkrieg, lightning war. It was begun and for many years successfully prosecuted by the huge espionage community of the Soviet
Union—the largest Intelligence system ever to exist.

The Soviet approach was unique in that while it employed all
traditional methods, its emphasis was less on professional Russian
spies than it was on subornation. The principle was to recruit
nationals of Britain, Germany, the United States, train them, and
have them serve Soviet overseers—'case officers'. The advantages
were obvious. Apart from the great length of time required to make
over a Russian so that he could pass as a man of Cornwall, a New
Yorker, a Würtemberger, there was the specific advantage of
requiring only one KGB case officer—rather like a pimp—controlling and guiding a cadre of nationals who, when caught, could
simply be written off.

There was nothing new in this, except that with the Russians it
was their main Intelligence ploy and while for many years Western
counter-Intelligence agencies were painstakingly searching for
Soviet spies, nationals of the U.S.S.R., restricted information by
the ton was being sent to Moscow by case officers who had in their
control natives of all non-Communist countries, *by the thousands.*

For over twenty years the Briton, Harold 'Kim' Philby, spied for
the Soviet Union while a high-ranking officer of M.I.6. Nor, when
he eventually fled behind the iron curtain did Philby's future with
the Russians seem much different from his past. He was assigned a
position with the Soviet disinformation agency, *Novosti,* whose
purpose was to promote secret subornation.

At the time Philby was engaged in spying from within M.I.6 his
Soviet contact was a very versatile KGB officer named Anatoli

Gorski, among whose aliases were Gromov and Nikitin. After Philby's defection these two became close friends in Moscow; that was during the period when Philby accused Great Britain of blatant and inexcusable spying.

The Philby story has been told many times. Here, in these pages, it needs recalling only to emphasize how adept the Russians became in the decades following the Second World War at infiltration, recruitment and subornation. Philby most certainly provided the KGB with lists of British spies, with names of the Britons liable to subornation and with all the secret material he could put his hands on, which would have been quite a bit considering his high position with British Intelligence.

His revealing blunders were not simply instances of carelessness —as when in Beirut he sought to recruit an Arab official to spy for B.I.S. when the Arab already was a British spy—they were also clear instances of something more sinister, but it was less the S.I.S. which uncovered Philby than it was the Lebanese secret service. They tracked down his clandestine double life, and the British took over—but none too well. Philby had no difficulty eluding S.I.S. shadows in late January 1963. He was next seen in Moscow's Red Square.

Somewhat earlier the same Soviet agent who had figured in Philby's life, Anatoli Gorski, also acted as KGB liaison between two other suborned Britons, Guy Burgess and Donald Maclean, whose tale is also well-known, and if Philby's treason appeared to arise from a psychiatric labyrinth, the Burgess-Maclean affair was unlike it without being any more admirable. Nor were the details as important as the fact that Burgess and Maclean were also Soviet spies while serving England in positions of trust. In fact Philby's friend Donald Maclean was a liaison official between British Intelligence and the United States Central Intelligence Agency.

He had been a Communist since about 1934, as had his associate Guy Burgess. What these men and Philby indicated even more than what their treason cost Britain in other ways, was that British security was incapable of meeting the challenge of innovative Soviet Intelligence.

It could apprehend such people as Harry Houghton and Ethel Gee, or the Americans named Cohen who masqueraded in England as Mr and Mrs Peter Kroger, individuals who were already suspect, but it seemed to have no protection against assault from within.

It certainly lagged in the field where the Soviets excelled— tangential espionage, the turning around of spies. It also lagged, more understandably, in recruiting Russians in their native land. There was a world of difference between Britain's open society and the controlled Soviet closed society. Recruitment within the U.S.S.R. was virtually impossible. It *was* accomplished, but very rarely. In comparison the Soviet Union planted networks in all the major countries and many of the minor ones. They recruited people ten years earlier in order to have a clerk of trust in the Foreign Office, M.I.6, or in an overseas embassy when one was needed. Meanwhile, they pressed their subornation programmes, steadily acquiring more native spies. They moved into areas where neither S.I.S. nor the C.I.A. had enough experience, manpower or funds to oppose them, and they did it with an *élan* not ordinarily associated with the Soviets.

They accomplished a great deal through their subornation programme, but while this was critically important to them, it was purely an espionage undertaking, secret, unknown to the general public, and their dedication to the overthrow of free governments required that they give at least equal time and effort to this other effort. Following the Second World War they demonstrated some expertise in peacetime agitation, but they were still rooted in old-time, hackneyed phrases and First World War ideology. But that would change as they moved through the 1950s to the 1960s and 1970s.

Following the Second World War they failed in attempts to discredit the United States rehabilitation scheme for Europe, called the Marshall Plan, and the establishment of the North Atlantic Treaty Organization (NATO). They then came forth with several publications purporting to be captured German war-time documents—which they undoubtedly were—full of clumsily inserted Communist alterations alleging secret infamies against Great Britain and the United States.

At about the same time the United States Department of State published a collection of documents from the German Foreign Office entitled *Nazi-Soviet Relations, 1939–1941*, edited by Eddie and Sontag, which considered the secret treachery against Poland by Hitler and Stalin, and while this was well received in the United States and abroad, the Soviets denounced it as a forgery.

And so, along with the secret espionage war which was then

expanding, there was now also to be a war of the 'paper mills'.

Soviet secret agents retaliated for *Nazi-Soviet Relations, 1939–1941* by photocopying the diary of the United States Military Attaché in Moscow, General Robert Grow, inserting such false statements as "War! As soon as possible" and publishing their 'exposé' under the title *On The Path To War,* under the innocent-appearing name of an Englishman residing in East Germany, Richard Squires.

Western Intelligence circles first knew of *On The Path To War* when it appeared in England and the United States, and it was indeed a clever 'exposé' of United States secret plans to attack the Soviet Union. The best Soviet effort thus far. After a quarter century of clumsy attempts to influence people through name-calling, U.S.S.R. Intelligence had learned how to combine a small truth and a big lie to create something uninformed people could believe. It was not a Soviet discovery. Joseph Goebbels, Hitler's tough, resourceful, crafty minister of propaganda, had developed this same capability to its zenith, but Goebbels was gone and his Soviet successors carried the post-war effort even farther.

United States reaction to *On The Path To War*, otherwise known as the Grow Diary, was to make public, excerpts showing where falsifications had been inserted. But the damage had been done. (General Grow was tried by court-martial on a charge of neglecting to protect restricted information—his own diary!) The United States, like Great Britain, was being rather consistently out-gunned in the war of the 'paper mills', but S.I.S. at least, was if nothing else, superbly adaptable. Almost before the furore had died away over the Grow Diary, a document known as 'Protocol M' appeared.

The sequence for Protocol M was roughly as follows: a German newspaper, *Der Kurrier* first published extracts on 14 January 1948. On 15 January 1948 British and United States newspapers followed with their own exposés.

Protocol M was more than a simple invitation to German workers to revolt against Allied authorities in the various sectors of Occupied Germany, it was a set of instructions how this should be done. For example, quoting from the text, the German workers were told that "Through persistent battle and in conjunction with the working class throughout Europe" they would "conquer the key positions in production" and that "This battle is not concerned with ministerial posts but is for starting positions for the final struggle for the liberation of the proletariat of the world. . . . The centres of the mass struggle are: (a) The Ruhr district and its production."

The document had every typical Communist phrase, appeal, and incitement. The complete text was published in the *New York Times* and aroused almost as much ire in the United States as the Zinoviev message had done a quarter century earlier.

Lending substance to Protocol M's authenticity, a crisis occurred in the Ruhr when 140,000 German workers inaugurated a twenty-four hour strike throughout the British Occupation zone, adding fuel to the already widespread belief that the Soviet Union was either embarking upon, or was shortly to embark upon, a nation-wide strike all across Germany using its Communist cadres as outlined in the Protocol to create a total condition of havoc and anarchy.

It was later said that the Ruhr strike was not Communist-inspired but was a protest against food shortages, nor could that allegation be proved any more easily than the parallel contention that the strike *was* Communist-inspired, but in either case it was fortuitous for the creators of Protocol M. Almost unbelievably fortuitous.

The Soviet Union denounced Protocol M as a complete forgery; as an Anglo-American device to discredit the U.S.S.R. Part of the evidence in support of this position appeared to be that while the British Foreign Office made copies available to several foreign governments prior to publication by *Der Kurrier*, none was sent to the Soviet government. Soviet military authorities in East Germany ridiculed Protocol M, through the *Taglicher Rundschau*, as did Radio Moscow, but, as with the United States position subsequent to the Grow Diary 'exposé', an attitude of defence was not adequate. The blow had been successfully struck, many people in Germany and elsewhere remained convinced that the Soviet Union was seeking to paralyse Germany through a labour uprising.

As to the authenticity of Protocol M, because its initial appearance was through Britain's Foreign Office, a fact which was easily established, there was not at first a lot of scepticism, but eventually, as in inevitable comparison was made between Protocol M and the much earlier Zinoviev letter, doubts arose.

An enquiry launched in the House of Commons elicited a terse response from the Foreign Office to the effect that "His Majesty's Government believe[d] this document to be genuine".

A lot of righteous indignation became acute embarrassment, then, because newsmen in particular disliked being used, and the entire affair was subjected to a lengthy and publicized investigation which not only hurt British Intelligence and the Foreign Office, but which thoroughly discredited Protocol M in Germany, and this was the curse of inexpert disinformation and propaganda in free societies. In Russia no such investigation would have been undertaken, nor allowed, in Great Britain it *was* allowed, was in fact encouraged, therefore the kind of amateurs responsible for Protocol M's faulty base could expect to be at least accused whether they were ever actually exposed or not, and in this case they were not. An Under-Secretary for Foreign Affairs, C. P. Mayhew, stated before Parliament that the Foreign Office had come by Protocol M through a reliable source, a German "not employed by His Majesty's Government".

It also transpired that this German by his own admission "was the author of the document". In mitigation, it was then weakly stated that "even if the document is not authentic, it has been compiled from authoritative Communist sources".

The agitation continued for some time, until it was discreetly allowed to die naturally, resulting in embarrassment to the government, without the full facts ever coming out. Nor was that necessary in the light of what had been uncovered; primarily that Protocol M, regardless of its bona fide sources, had not originated with the Russians.

As for the purported German author who was never named or prosecuted under the laws covering forgery and fraud, the government's position seemed reflected in Christopher Mayhew's statement that while the Foreign Office knew the "name of the German, but as . . . we cannot be certain he is the author . . . in these circumstances we cannot assume his guilt, and we do not, therefore, wish to expose him or his relatives to possible reprisals".

Was there ever a 'German author' of Protocol M? The answer to that along with other answers are not available. Was Protocol M acquired, as has been alleged, through normal Intelligence collecting channels? Conjecture suggests that it was not acquired, that it was created, and for a purpose; in retaliation for the whole series of U.S.S.R. psych-war techniques which until about 1961–2, were superior to anything S.I.S. or C.I.A. could provide.

But that situation began to change dramatically in the 1960s.

18

Coup And Countercoup

In most human endeavours someone is usually given credit either for a discovery or an improvement, and the Intelligence environment is not without its examples, although commonly, as with the C.I.A. which gives decorations not to be worn in public, credits are part of a secret, and must therefore also be secret.

Captain Winterbotham who contributed greatly to the successful secret history of the Second World War, was discreetly decorated and sent back to civilian life in south-west, rural England, one more veteran, but in his case bound by oath to remain silent about an affair, the Ultra project, which played a stirring part throughout the war and which contributed so greatly to the victory.

Occasionally credits, while minimized as in Captain Winterbotham's case, were also attributed erroneously, as appears to be the case with the war-time Special Operations Executive organization, "Churchill's daring plan to defeat Germany through sabotage, espionage and subversion." In the book, *Set Europe Ablaze*, by E. H. Cookridge, (Thomas Y. Crowell, New York) S.O.E.'s undertakings seem to leave an impression that it was S.O.E. which developed the Continental secret networks, when in fact it was the Secret Intelligence Service which established the initial espionage-sabotage organizations in Occupied Europe.

Credits in the field of Intelligence have never been easily ascribed even in instances where it has been thought proper to give credit. In war-time they were easily muted and afterwards, when given, while it was not widely or generally done, it was not as a rule done publicly.

A fair example would be the various sources accredited with suborning the most spectacular turn-around of recent times, that concerning the defection of Soviet GRU Colonel Oleg Penkovskiy.

What actually occurred was a brilliant bit of work inside the Soviet Union by an accomplished British secret agent, and without evidence to support the contention, it seems that this happened after S.I.S. had been signalled by the C.I.A. through its connections in Turkey that Penkovskiy was susceptible either as a genuine 'walk-in' or perhaps as a GRU-KGB 'plant', but which in any case the C.I.A., recently burned, chose not to exploit.

Penkovskiy was that most invaluable spy, the individual 'in place', the native of a hostile land whose bona fides are above reproach. The highly placed spy whose position makes possible the selective plundering of enemy top-secret information.

What former C.I.A. director Allen Dulles chose to call "volunteers for the West" meaning subverted individuals serving Western Intelligence from deep within Eastern Bloc countries, as well as from within the Soviet Union, have been the finest source of all top-secret material up until development of the sky-spy satellites, and even then, as a result of satellite limitations, the agent in 'deep cover' remains priceless.

Colonel Penkovskiy was a spy for British Intelligence, and later also for United States Intelligence, for about two years. His contact for the first part of that interlude was the British secret agent Greville Wynne, who was not only a consummate actor but who was also a humanist. Wynne's appraisal of the Russian was enlightening: "Oleg Penkovskiy was a most extraordinary man. . . . He was an intense man. He wanted not merely to give intelligence information, but to also let the people of Britain and the United States know about his motives. . . . He was bitter about the Soviet regime . . . he talked about its misdeeds and the sufferings or unhappiness of his friends." He was convinced the Soviet leadership was creating a vast military machine with which to launch a war when the opportune time arrived. He fiercely opposed this ideology and although he was disillusioned, he remained loyal to some principles which were not divorced from Communism.

On 11 May 1963 Oleg Penkovskiy was put on trial in a crowded room of the Soviet Supreme Court in Moscow. He was forty-four years old, married, a career officer, well-connected in the Soviet hierarchy, holder of military decorations for valour, the exact prototype of a Soviet careerist other Russians had been encouraged to admire and respect. Three days later he was shot to death after having been condemned for the ultimate offence: espionage against the Soviet State.

He had been a colonel of the military Intelligence organization

GRU, *(Glavnoye Razvedyuatelnoye Upravleniye)* the Chief Intelligence Directorate of the Soviet General Staff, although the Soviet prosecution said he was a reserve officer of artillery, a civilian in the employ of the State Committee for the Co-ordination of Scientific Research Work, and had no access to critical documents other than those having to do with research or economics.

But his trial stunned Soviet espionage people, particularly in Europe. It also created monumental headaches for the GRU and KGB leaderships in Moscow. Over 100,000 transcripts were printed and distributed as a warning to party groups within the country. To the outside world where interest was also keen, the Soviet leadership denounced Britain's part, and belatedly the United States' part, in what it called a vicious and underhanded attack against all peace-loving Russians.

General Serov, head of military Intelligence and part of his staff, were dismissed. Overseas operations were abruptly halted with key spies being hastily recalled. No one was certain of the extent of Penkovskiy's betrayal, but all officialdom knew he had been much more than a civilian employed by an obscure economic bureaucracy.

In fact Penkovskiy's revelations about Soviet military power, at that time second to the United States, was what enabled Washington to compel Premier Khrushchev to withdraw his missiles from Cuba in 1962.

He also knew of vital Soviet spying networks throughout the West, had had access to lists of spies, and knew about special subversion operations in Europe and the Americas.

All this information and more he certainly made available to British and American Intelligence.

At his trial mention was made of space secrets, top-secret military documents, information on Soviet strength in East Germany, anti-aircraft defences, recently perfected military hardware, and other items which must have destroyed the notion that Oleg Penkovskiy could only have provided S.I.S. and the Americans with scientific and economic information.

What particularly rattled Soviet leaders was that a man of such unimpeachable respectability could have been suborned. He was the highest-ranking defector of recent times.

How it was done seemed simple enough. A British businessman named Greville Wynne visited the U.S.S.R. in December 1960 as an advance representative for a group of British businessmen who were to explore avenues for reciprocal trade. Colonel Penkovskiy stated at his trial that he made the first move; he cultivated Wynne and when they were good friends he prevailed upon Wynne, the British businessman, to smuggle a packet of secret—and very incriminating—documents out of the Soviet Union, and to give them to British Intelligence when he reached home.

This occurred in early April 1961. One week later Penkovskiy also arrived in London, ostensibly in charge of a Soviet trade delegation. For twenty days, until his return to Russia, 6 May 1961, Oleg Penkovskiy met in secret at night with M.I.6 people and their C.I.A. counterparts.

Penkovskiy's earlier attempt to secretly defect to the United States through a Mediterranean C.I.A. contact, which had ended in refusal on the United States side, seemed to have left the colonel more favourably inclined towards the British. Nonetheless he was 'commissioned' a high officer of the United States armed forces, was provided with an appropriate uniform, which he wore in private quite often, and clearly considered himself a defector not a traitor.

His contact within the Soviet Union remained Greville Wynne— the businessman whose cover was good enough so that later at Penkovskiy's trial, it was only obliquely challenged. Penkovskiy's secret service contacts in London were agents Miles and Grille, plus two C.I.A. agents who preferred to be known under the pseudonyms of 'Oslaf' and 'Alexander'.

These agents of the West trained Penkovskiy in espionage techniques, provided him with a tiny camera and a radio transmitter, coaching him in masking and eluding, drilled him in successful techniques for quick escape, and sent him on his way back to Moscow.

A little later Wynne also flew to Moscow. He gave Penkovskiy thirty rolls of film and new instructions. When it became necessary for the colonel to visit London again he did so in connection with a Soviet Industrial Exhibition. He also met his M.I.6 and C.I.A. contacts, but to really appreciate Greville Wynne's "extraordinary man" it is necessary to follow him through a typical twenty-four hour period. First, he had shopping lists from friends and superiors at home to care for—no easy thing for a man with a language difficulty. He also had to avoid arousing suspicion at the Soviet Embassy where a GRU resident official was only part of the overall espionage and surveillance team. He had to impress everyone with his sincerity as part of the Industrial Exhibition, had to shepherd other Russians, was supposed to do as much industrial espionage as possible—and have six to ten-hour sessions at 'safe houses' with his S.I.S. and C.I.A. associates.

And he managed to do every bit of it with a smile. He was a gregarious man who did not drink much but enjoyed sightseeing and socializing. Each trip to the West seemed to deepen his interest and fascination. He made ready comparisons between closed and free societies, formed a number of friendships—one with Janet Anne Chisholm, wife of a member of the British Embassy staff in Moscow—others with additional Britons, and even a few Americans.

Janet Anne Chisholm was later a 'contact' in Moscow. He sent rolls of exposed film to S.I.S. through her.

He photocopied all manner of secret Soviet Intelligence documents, identified Soviet officials, presumably spies, from M.I.6 and C.I.A. photographs, passed along the gist of top-level espionage conferences he had attended, provided Western Intelligence with Soviet space and missile information, and co-operated in every way.

Presumably he also kept a journal at this time. More about that later. To his Western contacts he was 'Alex'. They were to use that designation when seeking a meeting with him. As time passed, while his original contact, Greville Wynne, remained pre-eminent, there were other contacts—probably too many of them—along with a number of drop-sites where Penkovskiy could leave messages and rolls of film to be sent to the West.

The British Embassy was aware of what was in progress. The Americans also had contacts, through their Moscow residency. Whether suspicion and disclosure came through one of these sources is moot, but both the GRU and the KGB were advanced, very adroit Intelligence concerns, and it was not improbable that through a spy either inside one of the Moscow embassies, or back in London—someone who was never uncovered, of the Philby, Maclean, Burgess or George Blake variety—a signal alerted Soviet Military Intelligence.

At any rate the colonel was already under surveillance when he passed more film to Janet Anne Chisholm in the first week of January 1962. He suspected it. In fact he told Wynne he was under suspicion, but he continued to spy. In July the colonel passed details of a Soviet missile to United States contacts. He also informed them he was being watched. The curious situation went on. Normally surveillance inside the U.S.S.R. was not this prolonged. But Penkovskiy was a war hero, a high officer, a man with excellent Party connections.

Nonetheless, after the New Year there was obviously only one way for the affair to end. The C.I.A. gave Penkovskiy a false passport with which he could presumably leave Russia if it came to flight. There were several other options under consideration, one involving a submarine in the Baltic Sea.

In April, always vigilant to the possibility of joining Soviet delegations going abroad, he sought to become a member of a book exhibition scheduled to visit the United States. He was not considered, and it was stated in his journal the reason was possibly connected with a search for his father, who had been an anti-Bolshevik soldier—a White Russian—at the time of the 1917 Revolution. Perhaps. It was also Soviet policy to block departure from the country of anyone under even the faintest suspicion.

Greville Wynne, whose repeated trips back and forth had certainly not gone unnoticed either, appeared again in July and met the colonel, who was by then under constant surveillance. The process of tabulating his personal contacts was already under way, also, the places he visited, the cafés, doorways, et cetera which were dead-drops. A collection of photographs was being put together by the State, and once, when he complained to a KGB officer that his perfectly normal contacts with foreigners were being jeopardized by obvious surveillance, he was assured it would stop, and of course it did not stop, it was intensified.

As time passed Greville Wynne's uneasiness became more apparent. He was an accomplished secret agent, his training going back to 1938, but in the variety of static situation he was now involved with, where the principal was under suspicion, he most certainly was also suspected. Once Soviet counter-espionage felt sufficiently confident, the denouement was simply a matter of time.

One day at the Peking Restaurant Wynne had a fright. Colonel Penkovskiy appeared, according to pre-arrangement, but instead of being relaxed and smiling, he curtly informed Wynne they were being surrounded by the 'neighbours'. (The Soviet Intelligence term—in Russian *sosedi*—for the KGB.)

Penkovskiy then led the way in a successful withdrawal, and later that same day when Wynne was at Sheremetyevo Airport awaiting the departure of his flight to London, several official cars arrived out front and Colonel Penkovskiy entered the waiting-room walking briskly. He told Wynne he must leave immediately, and not wait for his regular flight, after which he took Wynne's ticket to the clerk, and using his rank as a high GRU official arranged for Wynne to board a flight ready to depart for Copenhagen.

Penkovskiy's actions were subsequently called an occasion of self-sacrifice. Knowing as he had that the KGB was searching for Wynne he had seriously jeopardized himself helping Wynne leave the country.

As for the KGB, it had indeed lost Wynne, but only temporarily. He was watched after his return to London and when in connection with his cover as a peripatetic businessman he visited Budapest in the last week of October 1962, the Soviet secret service moved in.

On 2 November he was abducted and flown back to Moscow.

Some time earlier Colonel Penkovskiy had been arrested. According to the court transcript this occurred on 22 October. Both he and Wynne were confined at Lubyanka Prison, that notorious structure a short walk from the Kremlin, built like a fortress around a large square, called by Soviet Intelligence *apparatchiks* 'the Centre', more formally known as the complex at Dzerzhinsky Square.

Of course there was a flurry of excitement at the British and United States embassies, but this could have amounted to little in comparison to the sense of loss at the Intelligence levels.

Nor was it fruitful to confine the anxiety to the details of betrayal. What must have struck knowledgeable Western Intelligence people was that the colonel had been able to operate so well for so long, particularly after it had become clear he was under suspicion.

But the KGB was to be especially abstruse; carefully and very deliberately so, because 'Alex's' downfall was almost certainly not a result of his mistakes. He was engaged in a game in which his life was at stake, and no one knew it better than he did. Also, he was a skilled, trained counter-espionage official as well as a qualified GRU spy. As for Greville Wynne, someone in S.I.S. clearly erred in allowing him to re-enter the Communist sphere at Budapest so soon after his narrow escape from Moscow.

What seemed most likely was that Colonel Penkovskiy was probably spied upon by someone in London; someone he had no reason at all to suspect. However, as the days advanced at Lubyanka Prison where he and Greville Wynne were intently grilled, the question of apprehension faded into the background as the more critical question of personal survival loomed larger—for Greville Wynne. Oleg Penkovskiy's future had ended the day he was escorted to the Lubyanka cell. No Russian Intelligence official and this included the three former chief directors of State Security, who were jailed there, left alive.

Ultimately, because something of the kind was required, Soviet officialdom produced its equivalent to S.I.S.'s Montgomery Hyde or the C.I.A.'s Stephen J. Meade. His name was Gvozdilin, GRU Lieutenant-Colonel A. V. Gvozdilin. He was credited with exposing Penkovskiy and it was almost certainly a pure fabrication. Not entirely because Soviet Intelligence did not put forward Gvozdilin in this capacity until two years after Penkovskiy's execution, but also because his name did not figure in any way among the documents connected with the case prior to the trial, where he appeared for the first time on the staff of the prosecution. He was not mentioned, for example, in Penkovskiy's journal.

But his name was conceivably among the seven hundred Penkovskiy furnished the S.I.S. and the C.I.A. with, as belonging to individuals either directly or indirectly connected with the GRU. If so, that would still be unverifiable through normal channels this late —in 1979.

Between 1960, when the awkward U.2 spy-plane incident plunged United States-Soviet relations into one of their periodic and largely unpredictable slumps, and 1962 when Oleg Penkovskiy was taken into custody, the Soviet leadership had been reacting to one Western Intelligence success after another. S.I.S. for example, had eventually begun to operate according to the new rules. They learned well. These lessons were used as justification for increasing the Soviet armed forces, as well as the already top-heavy state security monolith, and Penkovskiy's defection added fresh fuel. The GRU's chief, General Ivan Serov and his daughter were close friends of Oleg Penkovskiy.

Worse, a few years earlier, in 1958, the KGB had uncovered another C.I.A. spy inside the GRU. Lieutenant-Colonel Yuri Popov, and then-Premier Khrushchev had ordered a ruthless housecleaning. Serov survived in 1958; in 1962 he did not, nor did most of his staff. He was replaced by fat General Petr I. Ivashutin, who was first Deputy of the KGB. From that point on the GRU had most of its department heads moved out, to be replaced by personnel from the KGB.

One of General Ivashutin's edicts prohibited GRU to employ anyone without first obtaining KGB approval.

The doubts about Military Intelligence which Yuri Popov engendered, were confirmed by the Penkovskiy defection. These events, along with such occurrences as the U.2 incident and other indications of successful infiltration and subornation brought to a head conditions which would have made it necessary for the Kremlin to invent a scapegoat, if the GRU had not existed.

The KGB moved against Military Intelligence employing the same tactics it used elsewhere. It penetrated GRU councils, planted its spies everywhere, tightened control from the top, was granted permission to supervise all GRU operations, and in particular to pass judgment on all GRU personnel going abroad. In effect the GRU became more than ever a KGB adjunct. But if Western Intelligence authorities were hopeful over the shake-up following Penkovskiy's execution they were premature. Soviet Intelligence had survived countless reorganizations, name changes, abrupt alterations at the leadership level, and the purpose as well as the dedication remained constant—had been constant for about a half century.

Otherwise, the after-shocks of the Penkovskiy affair reached far beyond Moscow. For Greville Wynne, sentenced to prison for eight years as an accessory and a spy, the future was indeed gloomy in 1962, but unbeknownst to him his S.I.S. employers in London had apprehended a Canadian businessman named Gordon Lonsdale who was in reality a native Soviet citizen, a GRU Lieutenant Colonel, named Konon T. Molody. In 1964 the Russians agreed to exchange Wynne for Molody, after Wynne had served less than a year of his sentence, thus a career in British Intelligence going back to 1938 was not to end in a Soviet prison after all.

Eight British Embassy personnel including Janet Anne Chisholm were ordered to leave the U.S.S.R., and five United States Embassy people were also expelled for complicity in the Penkovskiy affair.

Later, S.I.S. assisted Greville Wynne in writing his recollections, entitled *Contact On Gorky Street,* the purpose, so it was said, being to help Wynne recover financially from his travail, and perhaps that was at least a half-truth. However, in 1963 Harold 'Kim' Philby, with KGB assistance had also produced a book of memoirs in which he derided British Intelligence—which he had served for many years—therefore it was not entirely unrealistic to assume Wynne's book was supposed to offset the Philby book, as the war of the 'paper mills' continued.

Another publication to come out of the 'paper war' and the Penkovskiy affair was the supposed journal of Oleg Penkovskiy, aptly entitled *The Penkovskiy Papers*. This was edited and translated by Peter Deriabin, a KGB defector and C.I.A. associate, with a foreword by Frank Gibney, another individual whose interest in C.I.A. affairs seemed to have followed editorship with the United States *Newsweek* Magazine as well as having written four books on political subjects likely to be viewed as good propaganda-writing.

The Penkovskiy Papers were denounced by Victor Zorza, Soviet expert for both the *Manchester Guardian* and the *Washington Post*, as a forgery which "could have been compiled only by the Central Intelligence Agency".

Doubleday and Company were invited to show the original copy, and either would not or could not do so. Truy copy or false, *The Penkovskiy Papers* made a fortune for someone. It is doubtful if the aged mother Penkovskiy left behind, or the wife who bore his daughter 6 February 1962 (she was fifteen months old when her father was executed) would ever receive any of that money.

19

When All Else Fails

The success of British Intelligence in developing Oleg Penkovskiy, after the Central Intelligence Agency had side-stepped his first overtures, resulted in one of the best windfalls of the 1960s. But Intelligence information shares with vegetables a high degree of perishability. What Oleg Penkovskiy revealed in 1962 was losing relevancy a year or two later, primarily because his embarrassed countrymen began at once to re-vamp the areas he had penetrated as a Western spy. Also because the nature of much of that information was already in the state of change which scientific discovery has ensured for all Intelligence information over the past few decades. What had been vital in 1962 had ceased to be critically important just five years later. Ten years later its value lay in its utilization as reference source.

Perhaps the greatest blow arising from the defection of high-ranking people is to national prestige. 'Kim' Philby's perfidy created a storm of indignation throughout Great Britain, less it would seem because of the secrets he probably gave the Russians than because S.I.S., that vastly-respected invisible shield of the nation, turned out to have the same feet of clay as any other bureaucracy.

The fault here is simply that as a result of the secrecy which has over the centuries become such an entrenched aspect of all Intelligence work, average people along with presumably informed leaders, are prevented from obtaining the kind of knowledge they must possess, and are entitled to possess, in order to make value judgments, as well as to understand and appreciate what, precisely, the Intelligence function is all about.

No better example exists in Britain than along the well-travelled pathways of history. Where, then, has such an eminent historian as George Trevelyan pushed aside the barriers to the past sufficiently to allow correct conclusions concerning the monumental epochs, each one of which no more than externally reflected some concealed, successful Intelligence work? Not because Trevelyan was at fault but because an incorrect presentation of history has been the norm as a result of the ingrained secrecy, much of which had lost relevancy centuries before.

All the wars according to history courses have been won by generals, admirals, and latterly by air marshals, while in fact for every field-marshal such as Sir Douglas Haig, there have been Intelligence people, spies, analysts and co-ordinators. It is these people, whose task begins with the dangerous business of accumulation and ends with the finished product being respectfully placed upon the general's desk, who are responsible for the general's reputation—for better or for worse depending upon what use was made of Intelligence.

Napoleon was correct and history has borne him out; one good spy is worth an army corps. Granting that for obvious reasons almost no current Intelligence is suitable for publication, a considerable amount of it from centuries past can 'go public' in order to put into correct perspective the position of the Intelligence function as it has existed and continues to exist.

Not all Intelligence work is clandestine. In fact a small percentage of it fits that category even in wartime. For example, the historic D-Day invasion of 6 June 1944, endlessly chronicled by historians and such participants as General Eisenhower, was preceded by an incredible variety of Intelligence work including estimates of tides, wind velocity, phases of the moon, as well as brilliant groundwork in delusion and deception—all before there could be invasion. As a separate, valued contribution this secret side of D-Day has never been completely chronicled. What this amounts to then, is a lop-sided presentation of history, and those whose only contact with the past derives from history, deserve better.

Of course there are aphorisms that can be employed as though they explain the entire endeavour, such as a fifth century B.C. remark by one Sun Tzu, a contemporary of Confucius, to the effect that "knowledge of the enemy's disposition can be obtained only from men". Profound, and reasonably accurate providing "other men" is expanded to include collators of satellite information since most observations of alien "dispositions" are currently done from twenty miles aloft.

The news media, when it cannot avoid a topic which it has especially been barred from, uses euphemisms. Generally, probably because this is the best it can obtain, the public also uses them. But trite sayings even when accompanied by Kissingeresque winks, are not enough to help public understanding, while the alternative, some foreign government's well-planted disinformation, is not acceptable either.

A thoroughly experienced former S.I.S. officer, Sir Compton Mackenzie, once said that the most dependable Intelligence is obtained from sources "in the field", colloquially known as "eyeball Intelligence". Observation. No one could dispute that although "eyeball" has become "lens" and "in the field" has become "miles above the field", this type of succinct comment leaves reams to be added, which has historically been left unsaid. Therefore a 'Kim' Philby or a George Blake—or in the United States a Cohen, Whalen or a Greenglass— can arouse adverse public opinion on the grounds that no one ever really approves of a traitor, not even the people he has served, but what that type of individual actually amounts to is generally a temporary embarrassment—*as long as a nation is not at war.* A 'Kim' Philby shows that one Intelligence service has triumphed over another secret service, which is prestigious for the winner and humiliating for the loser. However in the public mind it can create a sense of catastrophe; a crisis situation arising from government's refusal to—beginning at the college level —establish guidelines for public understanding of one of the most basic and essential—and certainly one of the most ancient— activities dealing with national safety.

It would also help to dispel the illusion of the cloak and dagger, for while national objectives have always been subject to a defence against someone else's 'dirty tricks', and in some instances have required additional 'dirty tricks', most Intelligence work is concerned with the accumulation of vast amounts of information, political, economic, military, scientific and technical; concerns which do not require toppling regimes or assassinating tyrants. The problem arising from public misinformation in these areas comes from novelists of the Rebecca West variety who capitalize on a topic which the public finds fascinating and about which authors know almost nothing, except how to peddle books through formula-writing. (Rebecca West referred to Oleg Penkovskiy as a Soviet scientist.) This constitutes yet another reason why a public airing of the Intelligence function—of course not the secrets nor the 'work in progress'—is required.

At present the need for clearer public enlightenment than the kind presented through spy-thriller fiction is related to the power and absolute peril of modern weapons. Intelligence work has always been every country's first line of defence, but while in the past time was required to transport armies to areas of battle, currently, an 'enemy' can drop from the sky without a sound and cook every living human being within its vast radius leaving all buildings standing, all traffic signals still functioning, and all motors still running. It can do this without warning—unless capable Intelligence organizations are zealously active in the national interest: defence *in time.*

The few voices raised thus far in defence of the Intelligence function amount to no more than a weak signal. The deliberate secrecy of five thousand years, along with the opportunistic tommy rot of scores of writers who are solely concerned with selling stories, have been responsible for Intelligence work being placed in roughly the same category as crime. Since the existence of every living thing on this earth is more dependent now than ever before on valid protective Intelligence, it would reasonably appear that those living things are entitled to know *why* there is an Intelligence community, *what* its objectives are and *how* it can best achieve objectives.

On one hundred acres at Orford Ness, England, a complex electronic communication and surveillance facility enabled the West to monitor Soviet activity over a vast front, but since electronic detection devices generate the identical kind of amperage and wattage as do the foreign facilities they monitor, they too are vulnerable. The Orford Ness installation was eventually the target of successful Soviet jamming. Would disclosure of this facility, its purpose and its fate have antagonized the Britons it was designed to protect? Hardly.

In 1975 a ship passing through St George's Channel between Ireland and Wales, fouled several large cables, part of an Intelligence submarine-monitoring and detection system. A year earlier British Intelligence discovered Soviet sonar bins—large containers of very sensitive hydrophones—within the periphery of British coastal defences. Another of these sonar bins was washed ashore in Scotland near a submarine base.

The best possible utilization of Intelligence would be to alert people what to expect should they encounter anything which could be an Intelligence device. To ensure public support through enlightenment rather than alienate it through hidebound tradition. As for revealing to the 'enemy' how his sonar bins were detected—he knows perfectly well how it was done, because he has been making identical detections for several years, of other people's bins.

In the summer of 1972 a young couple named 'Jones' established a laundry and dry-cleaning business above the Evangelical Bookshop at College Square East, Belfast, Northern Ireland. The man, 'Bobby Jones', had as his territory the Dunmurray area. For several months he picked up and delivered laundry; the business did well in a modest fashion.

At 11.15 a.m. 2 October a blue Ford car drew close to the laundry van; a man carrying a sub-machine-gun alighted, fired a burst into the van while another man also armed with a light machine-gun stood watch, then the pair of gunmen drove away.

Inside the van 'Bobby Jones' died slumped over the steering-wheel. His name was not Jones, it was Stuart. He was a secret agent for Army Intelligence, and while his cover, the laundry business, was indeed camouflage, it was not entirely so.

'Jones'-Stuart's purpose was to pick up laundry in an area long thought to harbour 'Provos' of the Irish Republican Army, which was indeed laundered—by forensic experts to determine who had recently handled explosives or fired weapons.

The 'sister' of 'Bobby Jones' who had operated the laundry business with him was Sarah Jane Warke, a lance-corporal of the Women's Royal Army Corps. She was recalled to England and in 1973 was awarded the Military Medal. Her citation "for security reasons" did not specify why she was honoured.

Why not? The I.R.A. knew why, Sarah Jane Warke knew and presumably Queen Elizabeth who made the presentation knew, as certainly did the Intelligence community including the ultra-secret Army's Military Reconnaissance Force (MRF), which was not acknowledged to exist, as well as other armed service units. MRF in particular knew, because both Ted Stuart and Sarah Jane Warke had been attached to MRF when Stuart was assassinated.

Why should not the public also have known a year later, when Sarah Jane Warke got her medal that a young man of great courage had died in defence of his personal principles? Everyone but the public knew, although that situation would in time be corrected to the extent that printed news of Stuart's death would surface—but not in full detail, which is too frequently the case where an Intelligence connection has existed. Either the news is presented from just one side, or someone's trite comments are employed to maintain a cover of secrecy and ignorance.

Certainly there will always be areas of exceptional sensitivity exactly as there will always be areas of highly technical specialization, neither being available to simple explanations and therefore unlikely to be widely understood. Yet there is nothing including Einstein's theorem nor the vaster Godhead concept which has entirely eluded lucid presentation; whether everyone can understand or not, it has been possible to make presentations which *are* comprehensible to many, perhaps even *most* people.

It would be of great benefit if the Intelligence purpose was made a part of upper-level education. The discipline which has never been but a visible extension of Intelligence—history—has had entire curricula built around it. And there could be a fringe benefit: the greatest riddle of them all—is there an unbreakable code?—could perhaps be resolved by some natural *aficionado* who at present is feeding pigeons in Trafalgar Square on his noon 'break' from a Brompton Road shop.

The need for codes will never cease, notwithstanding the satellite sophistication which has to some extent lessened the use of ciphers —and also of other traditional espionage techniques. Black Chambers have never become *passé* nor will they as long as a need for communication exists. If a genuinely unbreakable cipher is ever perfected it will probably be the result of someone's genius who is not affiliated with Intelligence. In the past this has been true. The great mathematical minds which have come belatedly into the world's black chambers were not spies, first, nor even Intelligence-trained.

Secret writing is as old as religion, as old as diplomacy and deceit and all the great ideologies. A United States spacecraft launched in 1972, 'Pioneer 10', has on board a simple cipher designed to be decoded some time far into the future when Pioneer 10 comes into the atmosphere of another inhabited planet. The message explains where the spacecraft came from and what kind of people sent it.

The ultimate code would never be that simple and the need for insoluble codes is great. The National Security Agency (NSA) which is the most secret and technically advanced Intelligence service of the United States has, in specially constructed vaults, files of codes which could not be promptly broken. They will succumb in time. Computers can achieve incredible results. Each of these codes is the product of genius. Each was designed to avoid the common weaknesses of duplication and emulation. Most are not just elaborate, they are also very complicated. But they will in time succumb, as all codes do eventually.

S.I.S. pioneered several systems which, while all were not undecipherable, achieved their purpose quite well. One of these was the 'one-time pad'. Its secret was simply that a code was only used once, and afterwards the 'key' was burned.

It was breakable but first the interceptor had to possess the 'key', and since 'keys' were instantly destroyed, this procedure being the crucial factor in the use of 'one-time pads', resolving the codes had to be turned over to computers, and here again, without the 'key' computers could make almost endless comparisons and still not arrive at correct translations.

S.I.S. pads were simple and usually small enough to fit comfortably into the palm of a hand. Their simplicity went farther. Coding was done from a series of pages in a pad which offered random selections of numbers or letters taken either horizontally or vertically in a sequence previously agreed upon.

There was never any duplication and once a message was coded the 'key' page was removed from the pad and destroyed. At the other end the recipient deciphered, then also destroyed the page from his little booklet.

Some 'one-time pads' were printed on highly inflammable cellulose material so that they could be swiftly destroyed in an emergency. Some were elongated, about the length of a pencil, rolled into tight scrolls. Others were tiny booklets not much larger than a thumbnail. All of them depended totally upon two factors: no duplication, and destruction after use. These are simple procedures, but it has been known for some time that occasionally the surest way to outwit the most impressively awesome products of modern technology has been, not to devise even more complex devices, but to create such essentially simple ones as the 'one-time pads', which were not insoluble, they were instead quite simply based upon the ability of the human hand to hold a lighted match to a tiny printed page, something the most sophisticated computer could not do.

The British Intelligence Service's history, steeped in a colourful past, has been responsible for many of the great innovations which have over the centuries ensured safety for the realm and which have also ensured respect for B.I.S. from beyond the realm. If room for 'radical' improvement exists at all it must lie in the clear need for more public enlightenment. Not, as has been said before, in sensitive areas, but in other phases, and these are both very numerous, and touch upon nothing secret or restricted.

Finally, there is one additional point to be made in favour of greater public awareness. There has recently appeared a new computer telecommunication system which is capable of compiling a dossier on every person in Great Britain in an astonishingly short length of time. This Orwellian system arose from the technology employed as 'message switching', the means by which *all information in the nation* can be intercepted, instantly scanned, catalogued, and slotted into individual dossiers. This flood of information would include everything about every individual alive—food preferences, physical condition, bank accounts, debts, sexual preferences, shape, build, colouring, I.Q., education, weaknesses, even colour preferences and degree of honesty.

If S.I.S. were to acquire this system it would become more than a simple depository, as is the United States National Security Agency, it would also have the means to become the most awesome police and blackmailing institution in the nation. Privacy would be the first casualty and perhaps freedom would be the second.

There is apparently no such thing as an impenetrable Intelligence organization, nor any variety of ferrets as diligent in the pursuit of their objectives as espionage infiltrators.

Recently a fresh series of exposés in West Germany turned up Soviet and East German agents in high circles of government. Even Switzerland uncovered a Soviet spy in one of her foremost defence force officials, General Jean-Marie Jeanmaire, who had successfully delivered Swiss and NATO secrets to the Soviets for fifteen years beginning in about 1961, suggesting that Switzerland, like Great Britain, while supposedly in possession of adequate security and counter-measure precautions, was still vulnerable.

Every Western country from the largest (the U.S.) to the smallest (tiny Andorra on the highland border between France and Spain) has been a target of espionage infiltrators or, even more elusive,

Intelligence Spotters or Principal Agents, who are rarely spies themselves but who are masters at locating, selecting and recruiting natives such as General Jeanmaire for espionage work.

At any given time there are Soviet, American or British secret agents at work within the boundaries of one another's countries. The most skilful have either penetrated one another's Intelligence organizations personally, or they have recruited 'in place' natives, who have often been cleared by security and who are already employed with the Intelligence agencies of their native lands.

The extremely secret American National Security Agency (NSA) despite the most rigid security precautions (which include scrutiny even of *ancestors*!) has had at least two 'in place' native American spies for the Soviet Union in its employ who for several years passed extremely sensitive information to Moscow.

It also had two native Americans in its employ whose unimpeachable security credentials granted them clearance to handle the most top-secret documents—defect to the Soviet Union taking with them priceless Intelligence secrets.

In Great Britain nothing in recent times so corroded public confidence in the Secret Intelligence Services (S.I.S.) as the revelation that a top M.I.6 executive, Harold A. R. (Kim) Philby had spied for the U.S.S.R. for thirty years.

At one time, shortly after the Second World War, Philby was chief M.I.6 executive over all British Intelligence efforts against the Soviet Union. What he could not abrogate he informed Moscow about in advance.

He was responsible for the disappearance of a score of American and British agents sent into the Balkans through Albania, Italy, Turkey and Greece between 1949 and 1954, or until the projects were cancelled because of an obvious leak.

The incredible fact about Philby and at least one other British double-agent, Guy Burgess, was that there existed and had in fact existed for years, a definite, lengthy involvement with communism. For Philby this involvement began at Cambridge University as early as 1934. Subsequent to the Philby exposé it was this obvious flaw which especially aggravated Britons who, while willing to concede the possibility of an infiltration, were very annoyed that their eminently successful Intelligence service, outstanding for so many centuries, had not in all that time conceived an adequate protection for itself against this most commonplace variety of calamity—a traitor.

Other calamities had occurred, and were to occur subsequently, so along with Philby's exposé (he had been the protégé of M.I.6's masterful Second World War chief Sir Stewart Menzies), public faith was already at low ebb when additional causes for scepticism surfaced.

Two Britons of substance, a homosexual named Guy Burgess, a trusted diplomatic courier who was also an Intelligence agent, and his friend from the Foreign Office, diplomat Donald Maclean who had also learned about communism at Cambridge University, were also revealed as Soviet spies.

Burgess and Maclean were able to elude apprehension after disclosure, by a warning from Harold Philby who was in the United States when he turned up the revelation that they were both under suspicion and were being secretly investigated.

They—and later Philby—were able to escape through their connections with a high Soviet diplomat. Burgess and Maclean were spirited out of Britain through the contacts of Soviet Ambassador (who was also a KGB Major-General) Georgi Zarubin. It was Zarubin's call for a crack E and E (Escape and Evasion) team which resulted in the disappearance of Burgess and Maclean.

At no time within memory had S.I.S. suffered such a sequence of devastating defections.

The extent of damage to Western security was very serious, and a subsequent Soviet announcement that Philby had been awarded a coveted honour, the Red Banner Order "for outstanding service over a period of years" confirmed the worst fears of Western Intelligence officials. Philby had indeed passed thousands of priceless secrets to the Soviets.

Another British Intelligence officer, George Blake, who was suborned in Korea and who served loyally as a double-agent until he was also exposed and sentenced to prison, added still another albatross to those already being worn by S.I.S. when a Soviet E and E team got inside London's Wormwood Scrubs Prison and got Blake out. He later surfaced safe and sound in Moscow, an event which brought cries of outrage from all corners of Britain.

Blake as well as Burgess and Maclean having lacked Harold Philby's exalted Intelligence position had been able to deliver less to their Soviet controllers, but the public view was one of equal disapprobation for all four men, and mostly the outrage was directed against the Intelligence services. The treason itself was inexcusable, but that it had been permitted to happen was in the media view, equally bad. Some held it was even worse.

With abundant justification British newspapers milked every drop of sensationalism out of these lurid windfalls and each event, as well as each additional media tirade, augmented plummeting public confidence.

Nor was there any way to erect suitable defences. Yet there were several aspects of this treasonable epoch which quite escaped notice.

One was that during the time Kim Philby was siphoning off British secrets in wholesale lots—during the Second World War and shortly afterwards—Britain and the Soviet Union were allies and, at least theoretically, friends.

Had this condition not prevailed, had Britain and the U.S.S.R. been antagonists during that same period as indeed were Britain and Germany, then the consequences of Philby's perfidy would have been disastrous beyond imagining.

Philby's defection was without question an example of monumental treason scarcely paralleled in British history, and yet in the perspective of *these times*, it was less critical to Western survival than the defection of one atomic scientist such as Bruno Portecorvo, who disappeared while on a European holiday and turned up alive and well in Moscow in 1955.

Philby's revelations could not even in those earlier times have resulted in anything like a Soviet attack upon Great Britain regardless of how much the Soviets knew of Britain's plans and defences, because Britain's strong ally at that time, the U.S., had the atom bomb and the Soviet Union did not.

Thus Kim Philby's treachery, while inexcusable by all honourable standards, and as publicized as it was, really posed less of an actual threat than did Portecorvo's defection. Philby's betrayal involved secrets which were critical *at that time* to British and NATO security but they were very quickly outmoded, while Portecorvo's knowledge assisted Soviet scientists to perfect offensive weapons so terrible they remain to this day a lethal peril to every person in the free world.

Another aspect of the Philby, Blake, Burgess, Maclean interlude concerned a fact well known in Intelligence circles that the time was long past when the 'C' type Intelligence system of school ties (literally) and social acceptance could run S.I.S. or any other national Intelligence organization. Thus if Britain's traitors shook the faith of Britons in their Secret Services, they also ensured that no more Cambridge University old boys could jeopardize national security by taking in flawed loyalists.

But most pertinent of all was the commonly unsuspected perishability of Intelligence information. Despite those earlier eras of S.I.S. humiliation, and as disconcerting as all those shocking revelations were, the clear fact is that nothing spoils as quickly as secrets. Particularly technical information, the backbone of most Soviet input.

For example there has been an ongoing secret war between Soviet and Western ELINT (electronic eavesdropping) and COMINT (communcations monitoring) agencies for years.

As swiftly as one side develops a new, innovative sky-spy, or overview capsule, the other side makes every effort to either steal the plans or ambush a prototype, the result being that yesterday's Samos is *passé* and tomorrow's Space Shuttle will shortly be *passé*.

Literally, defence secrets change with the seasons. No government declassifies sensitive material within years of its having achieved a moribund state, but they all *could* declassify secrets which are ten years old or older. This is unless, of course, the secrets are still of value which they rarely are. However Intelligence organisations invariably say that they are in order not to have to part with even old and outmoded secrets.

The information Harold Philby delivered to the Soviets during his heyday as a double-agent has not been acutely pertinent for at least ten years. Not even the Admiralty secrets subsequently given to Soviet principal-controllers by William John Vassall, the Briton compromised by the KGB through photographs taken at a homosexual orgy in Moscow, were critical within a very few years after being revealed.

Much restricted information, such as the number of tanks or submarines a nation owns, can never be wholly accurate nor dependable. In 1976 Soviet tanks numbered 42,000. (U.S. tanks numbered 9,000.) One year later both these figures were invalid. However, since U.S. tank production has been a consistent 450 vehicles annually, while U.S.S.R. tank production has been a consistent 2,600 tanks annually, Intelligence estimators can arrive at close and reliable statistics for the years 1977 through about 1980.

But none of this is secret information even though both the U.S. and the U.S.S.R. maintain that it is.

Another great secret of the superpowers which is no secret at all is the matter of submarine fleets. The Soviet Union had 335 vessels. The U.S. had 118 vessels.

Between the years 1973–5 Soviet and U.S. submarine production was consistent, with U.S. production subject to slight fluctuations while U.S.S.R. production remained comparatively constant. It was therefore possible to predict each total submarine fleet, and yet the moment a top-secret figure was given, it became obsolete because additional vessels were added to the fleets.

What actually comes out of all this, and the Philby-type defection, is a damaging exposé which undermines trust and confidence in Intelligence systems, and this remains. But actually the result is far less critical than newspapers and some 'authorities' claim. Twenty years after Kim Philby's treachery he is still earning cover credits in magazines with each article resurrecting earlier and usually much older allegations of S.I.S. incompetence, none of which have been valid for a decade.

Presently the field of overflight spy satellites holds top priority in sophisticated espionage circles, and yet here more than in almost any recent category, the changes arrive almost before tea-time.

Thus the damage to M.I.6 and British Intelligence networks generally from the Philby affair was considerable, and at the time even seemed irredeemably disastrous—and it *was disastrous*—but so perishable are Intelligence secrets that even information acquired through someone like Kim Philby begins to stale the very next day after it is revealed, and its perishability increases thereafter by the day.

In later years British Intelligence services had fewer scandals, which would seem to indicate there has been a superior system developed to cover up, or some loopholes have been satisfactorily plugged.

At the same time the services have scored some major triumphs beginning with the Igor Penkovskiy affair of the 1960s and continuing on up to the present time, but almost inevitably there will be other penetrations and other defections. The ceaseless battle continues in silence; while *they* are boring in at home, *we* are boring in abroad. It is reasonable and fair to assume that as long as this tireless and enduring duel of wits is in progress, no other kind of duel—the shooting kind, for example—is very likely to break out. Meanwhile it might be well to bear in mind that for every Kim Philby affair which reaches public attention there are dozens of very successful secret campaigns being waged and being concluded which prudence prevents from ever reaching the newspapers.

Bibliography

This England edited by Merle Severy, National Geographic Society, Washington, D.C.

The Penkovskiy Papers Doubleday & Co., Inc., New York

CIA Diary by Philip Agee, Penguin Books, London

Gestapo by Edward Crankshaw, Putnam, London; Pyramid Books, New York

Great True Spy Stories edited by Allen Dulles, Harper & Row, New York

Battleground by Samuel Katz, Bantam Books, London

The Scourge Of The Swastika by Lord Russell of Liverpool, Cassell and Co. Ltd., London; Ballantine Books, New York

The War Within by Comer Clarke, World Distributors Ltd., London

The War Called Peace by Harry and Bonaro Overstreet. W. W. Norton Co. & Co., Inc., New York

World War II (Secret Intelligence) by Paul W. Blackstock, Quadrangle Books, Chicago

A Shortened History Of England by G. M. Trevelyan, Penguin Books, London

Codes And Ciphers by Peter Way, Crown Publishers, New York

KGB by John Barron, E. P. Dutton, New York

The Making Of A Spy by Raymond Palmer, Crown Publishers, New York

The Invisible World Of Espionage by Lauran Paine, Robert Hale Ltd., London

A Short History Of American Democracy by Hicks and Mowry, Houghton Mifflin Co., Boston

The CIA At Work by Lauran Paine, Robert Hale Ltd., London

Secret Intelligence Of The Twentieth Century by Fitzgibbons, Stein and Day, New York

Armageddon In The Middle East by D. A. Schmidt, John Day Co., New York

The Real War 1914–1918 by Liddell Hart, Little, Brown & Co., Boston

Master Of Spies by General Moravec, Doubleday & Co., Inc., New York

The First World War by General R. Thoumin, G. P. Putnam's Sons, New York

Foreign Policies In A World Of Change, Black and Thompson, Harper & Row, New York

History Makers the fortnightly magazine, various editions, Marshall Cavendish, Sidgwick & Jackson, London.

History Of The Second World War edited by Liddell Hart, Purnell & Sons Ltd., London

Crusade In Europe by Dwight Eisenhower, Doubleday & Co., Inc., New York

Set Europe Ablaze by E. H. Cookridge, Thomas Y. Crowell Co., Inc., New York

The Ultra Secret by F. W. Winterbotham, Harper & Row, New York

The German General Staff by Walter Goerlitz, Praeger Publishers, Inc., New York

Hitler, A Study In Tyranny by Alan Bullock, Bantam Books, Inc., New York

The C.I.D. And The F.B.I. by R. Harrison, Corgi Books, London

Germany And The Next War by von Bernhardi, Longmans, Green & Co., New York

The Armada by Garrett Mattingly, Houghton Mifflin Co., Boston

From Lenin To Malenkov by Hugh Seton-Watson, Praeger Publishers, Inc., New York

In Flanders Fields by Leon Wolff, The Viking Press, New York

Inside The German Empire by H. B. Swope, The Century Co., New York

Star Of Empire by W. B. Wilcox, Alfred A. Knopf, Inc., New York

Additional sources for material on relative events, plus several biographical vignettes, and a considerable amount of inadvertent material, along with sources which added to the whole by contributing only a note, all of which would have tediously lengthened the bibliography without serving any other purpose, have been omitted.

Index